Basic Cookery

Basic Cookery

by Jennie Reekie

TREASURE PRESS

Photographs on pages 11, 15, 17, 21, 24, 65, 85, 119 and 123 by Bryce Attwell
Frontispiece: Store-Cupboard Casserole (Photograph by Lawry's Foods Inc.)

First published by Octopus Books Limited as
Popular Cookery for Young People

This edition published by Treasure Press
59 Grosvenor Street
London W1

© 1973 Octopus Books Limited

ISBN 0 907407 28 5

Printed in Hong Kong

CONTENTS

WEIGHTS AND MEASURES

All measurements in this book are based on Imperial weights and
measures, with American equivalents given in parenthesis.
Measurements in weight in the Imperial and American system are
the same. Measurements in volume are different, and the
following table shows the equivalents:

Spoon measurements

Imperial	U.S.
1 teaspoon (5 ml.)	$1\frac{1}{4}$ teaspoons
1 tablespoon (20 ml.)	$1\frac{1}{4}$ tablespoons (abbrev: T)

Level spoon measurements are used in all the recipes

Liquid measurements

1 Imperial pint	20 fluid ounces
1 American pint	16 fluid ounces
1 American cup	8 fluid ounces

Metric measures: for easy reference

$1\frac{3}{4}$ pints (working equivalent)	1 litre
1 pint (working equivalent)	$\frac{1}{2}$ litre
1 lb. (working equivalent)	$\frac{1}{2}$ kilogramme (500 grammes)

INTRODUCTION

Unfortunately the idea that Steamed Stuffed Cod and Creamed Carrots are the ideal fare for the inexperienced cook still seems to linger on, and it is sometimes hard to find interesting recipes which are not too complicated and do not baffle the novice with strange-sounding terms. None of the recipes in this book are difficult, but they are intended for people who want to cook, rather than open four cans and mix them all together, although use is made of convenience foods where practicable.

The first few pages deal with equipment and the store-cupboard and should be of particular interest to those just starting to live away from home. If you are a complete beginner I would suggest that you sit down and actually read the entire chapter on basic recipes and methods as these really are the basis of so many other dishes.

The remainder of the book is divided into four chapters, Meals for One and Two, Supper Dishes, Slimming and Entertaining. The first two contain everyday recipes, the Slimming is self-explanatory, and the Entertaining chapter covers dinner and buffet parties, and a few tea-time recipes as well. Whether you are still at school and living at home, are living in a bedsitter or flat, or are newly married and suddenly faced with having to cook a meal every night, I hope it will help you.

Food Storage

The contents of your store-cupboard will of course depend on how much space you have available, especially if you are living in a bed-sitter, the amount of cooking you do, and the number of people for whom you usually cater.

Storage containers:

One of the biggest problems in any store-cupboard, whatever size, is half-empty packets of sugar, rice and flour which have an uncanny knack of falling over and spilling their contents. If you do not want to go to the expense of buying storage jars, these can be kept in ordinary large screw-topped jars, the sort instant coffee comes in, or in large well washed tins, which can be covered with a foil top. You can either leave these jars and tins as they are, or cover them with a self-adhesive plastic covering. Perishable foods, such as butter, milk and bacon should, preferably, be stored in a refrigerator. If you do not possess a refrigerator, these foods should only be bought in small quantities. Storing fresh meat, especially in hot weather, without a refrigerator is almost impossible, but it will keep for up to 36 hours in a marinade which will not only keep the meat fresh, but will tenderize it and improve the flavour.

Basic Marinade:

Mix together 3 tablespoons ($3\frac{3}{4}$T) oil, 3 tablespoons ($3\frac{3}{4}$T) vinegar or lemon juice, dash Worcestershire or soy sauce, a chopped onion or crushed clove of garlic, if liked, and seasoning. Add the meat to the marinade and leave to soak, turning occasionally.

The Store-Cupboard

The Bare Essentials:
Flour
Sugar
Rice
Spaghetti
Oil
Vinegar
Sauces, such as Worcestershire and soy
Lemon juice in plastic lemons
Stock cubes, chicken and beef
Concentrated tomato purée in tubes
Dried mixed herbs

Salt, pepper and mustard
Canned tomatoes
Canned new potatoes
Canned meat e.g. minced beef or steak
The More Comprehensive Cupboard
This should contain all the items listed above, plus some or all of these:
Self-raising (all-purpose) flour
Cornflour (cornstarch)
Sugars, castor (superfine), granulated and soft brown
Dried fruit e.g. currants, sultanas
Packet(s) quick dried peas and beans
Packet dried onion flakes
Packets of soup
Packet(s) instant potato
Instant dried milk powder
Powdered gelatine (gelatin)
Honey
Golden syrup
Jam
Chutney
Canned meat e.g. tongue, ham
Canned fish e.g. salmon, tuna
Canned soups
Canned vegetables e.g. sweet corn, carrots, mushrooms
Canned fruits e.g. apricots, peaches, mandarins, pineapple
Dried herbs and spices e.g. dill, thyme, tarragon, cinnamon, nutmeg

Fresh Herbs

Whilst dried herbs give very good results, the use of fresh herbs will
improve your cooking immeasurably. Fresh parsley, which can generally
be bought throughout the year, will keep for a week if placed in a cup
containing cold water. Few herbs are difficult to grow and they will flourish
inside, so it is not essential to have a garden. All sorts of different "herb
gardens" are now available either as seeds or small plants, and if you are a
keen cook, it is well worth trying to grow these. Some herbs, such as
rosemary and chives will grow very well from a cutting, so if you have any
friends who will part with some, this is a much cheaper way of growing them.

Kitchen Equipment

To be a good cook it is not necessary to have a vast range of kitchen equipment, and it is amazing how well one can manage with only a very few items, provided they are the right ones.

The Bare Essentials:

1 knife – it is worth buying a really good knife for chopping as it will last for years.

1 knife sharpener – it is important to remember that you are more likely to cut yourself on a blunt knife, which you will have difficulty using, than on a sharp knife.

1 potato peeler – this is useful for peeling not only potatoes, but also carrots and apples.

1 grater – buy one with two or three different sizes on it.

1 chopping board – this can be just a piece of well scrubbed wood and can also be used as a bread board.

1 balloon egg whisk – for whisking eggs and cream

1 or 2 wooden spoons

1 large mixing bowl

1 small basin

1 frying pan

1 large saucepan

1 medium-sized saucepan

1 small saucepan

1 large sieve which can also be used as a colander

KITCHEN EQUIPMENT, SHOWING MAYONNAISE IN PREPARATION

A More Comprehensive List

The amount of equipment you can have is of course limitless, provided you
have sufficient space to keep it. Electrical equipment, such as mixers and
blenders, have not been included here, which is a list of the most usual
(and useful) basic equipment.

Saucepans and casseroles—you can almost never have too many of these.
As far as saucepans are concerned, it is best to buy good quality aluminium
ones as these will last for years, and are generally easier to clean. Non-stick
pans are a great boon but it is most important to follow the manufacturer's
instructions regarding their use and cleaning.

Kitchen tool set—including a ladle, palette knife, potato masher and fish
slice

1 roasting tin

Cake tins—One tends gradually to acquire things like this. Useful types and
sizes are 7- and 8-inch round cake tins, preferably one with a loose bottom
and one without, square cake tins and sandwich tins, and a 2 lb. loaf tin.

Flan rings—an 8-inch flan ring is the most useful size to have. China flan
dishes, such as the one pictured on page 29, not only look attractive, but are
also very useful.

1 mincer

1 pair of scales

1 measuring jug or cup

a selection of mixing bowls and basins

different sized knives

1 pastry brush

1 pair of kitchen scissors

1 lemon squeezer

1 rolling pin

1 pepper mill

1 garlic press

Putting Disasters Right

Even the most experienced cook has disasters from time to time, but provided one does not panic, it is often possible to save the day. However, in case of total disasters, it is a good idea to have a few spare cans of vegetables, meat, fruit and dry ingredients, such as spaghetti, so that you can quickly make up something else, such as Spaghetti Bolognese.

Lumpy sauces: Take the pan off the heat and, using a balloon whisk, whisk sharply.

Sauces or casserole too thin: Blend a little cornflour (cornstarch) with a few tablespoons of cold milk or water. Stir in two or three tablespoons ($2\frac{1}{2}$–$3\frac{3}{4}$T) of the hot liquid, then pour into the pan and stir well. Boil for about 2 minutes to cook the cornflour.

Casserole or soup too salty: Add 2 or 3 peeled and sliced potatoes. Allow them to simmer for about 10 minutes, then remove from the pan.

Casserole or stew is burnt; Do not stir; pour into a fresh casserole or pan. Add curry powder, chilli powder, Worcestershire sauce, or soy sauce to disguise the burnt taste.

A filled flan case breaks when you put it on the serving dish: If it is a savoury flan, cut it into portions and put plenty of watercress on the dish. If it is a sweet flan, put the filling into a shallow serving dish, crumble the pastry over the top and sprinkle with icing sugar or grated chocolate.

The top of a cake is burnt: Carefully take off the burnt edges and top with a fine grater, then sprinkle the cake with icing sugar before serving.

Rice or spaghetti has been over-cooked and is sticking together: Turn into a large sieve or colander and wash very well in cold water to remove all the starch. Heat a good knob of butter in a pan, add the drained rice or spaghetti and toss in the butter until piping hot.

Frying pan or pan of deep fat catches fire: Turn off the heat, cover the pan with a lid and very carefully take the pan to an empty metal sink, open window or back door. *Do not pour water over it.*

BASIC RECIPES AND METHODS

Roasting Meat and Poultry

Roasting is one of the simplest methods of cooking meat, and one of the most delicious. Before cooking the meat should be placed in the roasting tin, preferably on a grid if you have one, brushed or spread all over with lard, cooking fat (shortening), butter, margarine or oil and lightly seasoned with salt and pepper. During cooking the fat from the meat tin should be spooned over the joint two or three times; this is known as basting and keeps the joint moist and an even brown. The meat or poultry should first be placed into a hot oven, 425°F., Gas Mark 7 for 20 minutes, then the heat should be lowered to 375°F., Gas Mark 5 for the remainder of the cooking time.

Timing
The joints suitable for roasting are given, with timing, below.
Beef: For rare beef allow 15 minutes for every lb. meat and 15 minutes over. i.e. for a 4 lb. joint allow $1\frac{1}{4}$ hours.
For medium beef allow 20 minutes for every lb. and 20 minutes over.
For well done beef allow 25 minutes for every lb. and 25 minutes over.
Lamb: Allow 25 minutes for every lb. and 25 minutes over.
Pork: Allow 30 minutes for every lb. and 30 minutes over.
Veal: Allow 30 minutes for every lb. and 30 minutes over.
Chicken: Allow 20 minutes for every lb. and 20 minutes over.
Note: If you are stuffing the meat or poultry, you must add the weight of the stuffing, i.e. if you have a 5 lb. chicken and you use 1 lb. stuffing, the joint must be roasted for 2 hours 20 minutes.

Cuts of Meat

Beef
Prime cuts suitable for roasting: Fillet, sirloin, rib, top rump, topside
Prime cuts suitable for grilling or frying: Fillet, rump, entrecôte, T-bone, minute
Cheaper cuts suitable for stewing or casseroling: Chuck, buttock, skirt, neck, flank, shin

Lamb
Prime cuts suitable for roasting: Leg, shoulder, best end of neck, loin; breast can be slow roasted
Prime cuts suitable for grilling or frying: Loin or chump chops, best end of neck cutlets
Cheaper cuts suitable for stewing or casseroling: Middle and scrag end of neck, fillet, breast

Pork
All joints of pork can be roasted: Leg, bladebone, loin, spare rib; hand, spring and belly are inexpensive joints of pork for roasting
Prime cuts suitable for grilling or frying: Fillet, loin and spare rib chops

Veal
Prime cuts suitable for roasting: Top leg, loin, best end of neck, shoulder and breast
Prime cuts suitable for frying or grilling: Fillet, loin chops
Cheaper cuts suitable for stewing or casseroling: Breast, knuckle, pie veal

Slow Roasting

Some of the less tender joints, such as breast of lamb and veal are more tender if they are slow roasted. Put the meat into a moderate oven, 350°F., Gas Mark 4 for the entire cooking time. Allow 20 minutes per lb. more than if roasting as normal.

SPARE RIBS OF PORK WITH BARBECUE SAUCE

Foil Roasting

Roasting meat in foil reduces shrinkage, keeps in all the meat juices and helps to keep the oven clean. Prepare the meat in the usual way, and wrap in foil. There is no need to baste the meat, but the foil should be opened out during the last 20 minutes of cooking to allow the meat to brown. Meat roasted in foil takes longer, so allow an extra 10 minutes per lb. to the timings given on page 14.

Making Gravy

Good gravy can make a roast joint superb, so it is worth taking a little trouble to make it well. The very best results are obtained if you make it in the meat tin with the sediment left from roasting the joint, but if you are entertaining and want to make the gravy in advance, you can make it in a saucepan with a tablespoon ($1\frac{1}{4}$T) of the fat from the meat pan.

If making the gravy in the meat tin, pour off all but 1 tablespoon ($1\frac{1}{4}$T) of the meat fat. Put the tin over a very low heat on the top of the cooker and add 1 tablespoon ($1\frac{1}{4}$T) flour. Blend well and stir until the flour turns pale brown. Remove from the heat and gradually stir in $\frac{1}{2}$ pint ($1\frac{1}{4}$ cups) water and $\frac{1}{2}$ stock cube or, preferably, stock or liquid in which green vegetables have been cooked. Return the tin to the heat and bring to the boil, stirring all the time. Season with salt and pepper and add a few drops of gravy browning if liked. For special occasions, the gravy will be improved if you add 1–2 tablespoons ($1\frac{1}{4}$–$2\frac{1}{2}$T) sherry or port.

Roasting Potatoes

Peel the potatoes and cut up if large. Put into a pan of salted water, bring to the boil and cook for about 8 minutes. Strain. Heat 2–3 oz. ($\frac{1}{4}$–$\frac{3}{8}$ cup) lard or cooking fat (shortening) in a tin in the oven. Add the strained potatoes and turn in the hot fat until they are evenly coated. Cook above the meat for about 1 hour so that they are crisp and golden brown.

Grilling (Broiling)

Grilling (Broiling) Meat
Grilling (broiling) is a fast method of cooking and only the very tender cuts of meat can be successfully grilled (broiled). The grill (broiler) should be heated for at least 2 minutes before the meat is placed under it, so that the surface of the meat is sealed quickly by the heat. Before grilling (broiling), either brush the meat with melted butter or margarine or with oil, or dot with small pieces of butter or margarine. Season with salt and pepper, or for extra flavour, with a pinch of garlic salt or dried or fresh herbs.
Place the meat on the rack in the grill (broiler) and grill (broil) for 3 minutes. Turn the meat, using either a pair of tongs or two spoons (do not pierce the meat with a fork) and grill (broil) for 3 minutes on the second side. Either reduce the heat of the grill (broiler) or lower the position of the grill (broiler) pan and complete the cooking time. Baste the meat once or twice with the fat which has dripped into the pan.
Vegetables, such as tomatoes and mushrooms, can either be placed on the rack with the meat, or under the rack in the grill (broiler) pan.
Cooking times:
Rump steak, about $\frac{3}{4}$ inch thick: Rare, 6 minutes; Medium, 10 minutes
Lamb chump chops: 12–14 minutes
Lamb neck cutlets: 8–10 minutes
Pork loin chops: 15–20 minutes
Chicken quarters: 20–25 minutes
Sausages: 12–15 minutes

Grilling (Broiling) Fish

Almost every sort of fish can be successfully grilled (broiled). The preparation and method of grilling (broiling) is the same as for meat (above) but the rack should first be brushed with melted butter or margarine so that the fish does not stick.

Thin fillets of fish do not need turning and when grilling (broiling) fish it is especially important to baste well during cooking or the fish will become dry.

Cooking times:
Thin fillets: about 5 minutes
Thicker fillets: 8–9 minutes
Thick steaks or small whole fish e.g. trout: 10–12 minutes

Shallow Frying

Frying meat

Frying is another fast method of cooking for which only tender cuts are suitable. Heat the fat in a frying pan; this can be cooking or olive oil, cooking fat (shortening) or butter or margarine. When using butter or margarine, however, about 1 tablespoon ($1\frac{1}{4}$T) oil should be added to prevent the fat from burning and browning.

When the fat is hot, put the seasoned meat into the pan and cook at a high temperature for about 2 minutes. Turn, using tongs or two spoons, and cook at a high temperature for 2 minutes on the other side. Lower the heat and continue cooking until tender.

Cooking times: As grilled meat (see page 19)
Liver: 6–8 minutes
Escalopes of veal: 8–10 minutes

Frying Fish

Frying is probably the most popular method of cooking fish. Before cooking most fish is either lightly coated in flour, or dipped in egg and breadcrumbs. Cook as for meat (see above).

Cooking times: As grilled fish (see above)

GRILLED FISH WITH TOMATOES AND MUSHROOMS

Mayonnaise

2 egg yolks
$\frac{1}{2}$ teaspoon dry mustard
$\frac{1}{2}$ teaspoon salt
pepper

$\frac{1}{2}$ pint ($1\frac{1}{4}$ cups) oil
2 tablespoons ($2\frac{1}{2}$T) wine
vinegar or lemon juice

If possible have all the ingredients at room temperature. You can make mayonnaise with eggs straight from the refrigerator but there is a much greater chance of it curdling. Beat the egg yolks with the mustard, salt and pepper. Using either a balloon whisk or a wooden spoon, whichever you find easier, gradually beat in half the oil, drop by drop, until the sauce is thick and shiny. Beat in 1 tablespoon ($1\frac{1}{4}$T) of the vinegar or lemon juice then beat in the remaining oil. At this stage the oil can be added a little more quickly. Add the remaining vinegar or lemon juice when all the oil has been incorporated.

If you want to thin the mayonnaise down a little, you can add some lemon juice, a little single (light) cream or 1–2 teaspoons hot water.

The thick mayonnaise can be put into a screw-topped jar or other suitable container and kept in the refrigerator for about 2 weeks. If you added the oil too quickly at the beginning and the mixture curdles, beat another egg yolk in a clean basin and beat in the curdled mixture, a teaspoon at a time.

White Sauce

1 oz. (2T) butter or margarine
  1 oz.(2T)flour

$\frac{1}{2}$ pint ($1\frac{1}{4}$ cups) milk or milk
  and fish, vegetable or
  meat stock
salt and pepper

Melt the butter, or margarine in a saucepan. Stir in the flour and cook for about a minute over a low heat. This mixture of fat and flour is known as "roux". Remove the pan from the heat and gradually stir in the milk or milk and stock. Return to the heat and bring to the boil, stirring all the time. Cook for about 3 minutes until the sauce has thickened. Season to taste.

French Dressing

The ingredients in French dressing and the proportion of oil to vinegar are very largely a matter of personal taste, but this recipe is a good basic one.

1 tablespoon ($1\frac{1}{4}$T) distilled
  malt, or wine vinegar
2–3 tablespoons ($2\frac{1}{2}$–$3\frac{3}{4}$T) corn
  or olive oil

$\frac{1}{4}$ teaspoon made English
  mustard or French mustard
pinch sugar
salt and pepper

Put all the ingredients into a screw-topped jar and shake well until blended. French dressing will keep for months and it is a good idea to make up about $\frac{1}{2}$ pint ($1\frac{1}{4}$ cups) and store it. Always shake well before using.

Separating an Egg

First crack the egg in the middle, either on the edge of a bowl or with a knife. Then, holding the egg in both hands, carefully pull the shell apart so that the yolk moves into one half of the broken shell and the white drops into a bowl. To remove the last of the white, carefully transfer the yolk from one half shell to the other a couple of times, allowing the white to fall into the bowl. If you need more than one egg white for whisking, it is advisable to crack each egg into a separate basin or cup and then transfer it to the mixing bowl, so that if you should make a mistake and drop yolk into the white, two or three egg whites are not wasted.

Whisking Egg Whites

The egg whites should be put into a clean, dry bowl. There should not be any specks of yolk at all; if there are, remove these with a teaspoon or the corner of a piece of kitchen paper. Using either a fork (this takes a very long time), a balloon whisk or rotary beater, whisk the eggs very hard until they stand in soft peaks and you can turn the bowl upside down without the mixture falling out.

Cooking Green Vegetables

The way in which green vegetables are cooked is very important, for if the vegetables are cooked badly or overdone, they will not only taste unpleasant, but will lose many of their valuable vitamins. The vegetables should first be prepared according to type and washed in cold water. Put about 2 inches of water into a saucepan with 1 teaspoon of salt and bring to the boil. Add the vegetables to the pan over a high heat then, as soon as the water is boiling again, cover the pan, lower the heat and continue cooking. The vegetables should be removed from the heat and drained when they are *just* tender as they then retain the maximum vitamins.

Whipping Cream

Only double (heavy) cream, whipping cream or a mixture of at least half double (heavy) and single (light) cream can be used for whipping. Care should be taken when whipping double (heavy) cream on its own as it is very easy to over-whip and end up with a buttery mixture. If you have not had very much cookery experience, it is best to use a fork for beating as there is then little chance of over-whipping. If using whipping cream or a mixture of double (heavy) and single (light), use a balloon whisk or rotary beater. The cream should be whipped until it just holds its shape and stands in soft peaks, then *stop* as the cream will thicken up a little more on standing.

Using Gelatine (Gelatin)

People often think that gelatine (gelatin) is difficult to use, but provided you follow these basic directions, you should not have any problems. The most common form of gelatine (gelatin) is the powdered variety which comes either in $\frac{1}{2}$ oz. envelopes or loose with a $\frac{1}{2}$ oz. scoop. To set 1 pint ($2\frac{1}{2}$ cups) of liquid you will need $\frac{1}{2}$ oz., and to set up to 1 pint ($2\frac{1}{2}$ cups) thickened mixture (such as a cream or mousse) you will need 2 teaspoons.

To prepare $\frac{1}{2}$ oz. (1 envelope) gelatine (gelatin), put 4 tablespoons (5T) cold water into a basin and sprinkle over the gelatine (gelatin). Leave for 5 minutes for the gelatine to soften, then stand the basin over a saucepan of very gently simmering water and leave until the gelatine (gelatin) has completely dissolved. Use as directed in the recipe.

To Make a Flan Case

Place a flan ring on an upturned baking tray, or use a sandwich tin. For a 6-inch flan you need 4 oz. (1 cup) pastry, for a 7–9 inch flan you need 6 oz. (1½ cups) and for a 10–12 inch flan you need 8 oz. (2 cups) pastry.

Roll the pastry out evenly into as neat a circle as possible, about 2 inches larger than the diameter of the flan ring. Using the rolling pin for support, carefully lift the pastry into the flan ring. With your index finger, press the pastry down into the flan ring and, if using a fluted flan ring, into the flutes, To neaten the edge of the flan, starting from the centre, roll away from you so that the excess pastry is cut off leaving a neat edge. Turn the flan round and repeat the process. Either fill the flan and bake, or bake blind.

To Bake a Flan Case Blind

Put a sheet of greaseproof (waxed) paper or foil, about 4 inches larger than the diameter of the flan, into the bottom of the flan case. Fill the flan with dry crusts of bread, beans or rice. Put into a moderately hot oven, 400°F., Gas Mark 6, and bake for 10–15 minutes or until the pastry is set. Remove the greaseproof (waxed) paper and bread, beans or rice and bake for a further 5–10 minutes to dry out the base.

If using baking beans or rice they should be allowed to cool, then put into a suitable container. They can then be used again.

Note: If you are using a china flan dish like the one illustrated opposite, you will probably find that the flan case takes slightly longer to cook and that fillings also take longer to set. This is because the china does not transmit the heat as fast as tin.

DUTCH LEEK AND MUSHROOM FLAN (Photograph by Dutch Dairy Bureau)

Short Crust Pastry

8 oz. (2 cups) plain flour
pinch salt
4 oz. ($\frac{1}{2}$ cup) fat, this can be
butter, margarine, or a
mixture of margarine and
cooking fat (shortening)

pinch salt
about 3–4 tablespoons ($3\frac{3}{4}$–5T)
cold water

Sieve together the flour and salt. Cut the fat into small pieces. Rub the fat lightly into the flour using your fingertips, until the mixture resembles fine breadcrumbs. Add the water and bind the mixture using a knife, so that it clings together leaving the sides of the bowl clean. Put on to a floured board or working surface and knead *very lightly* so that you have a smooth, round ball. Roll out the pastry and use as required.

It is important when making short crust pastry that the mixture is not overhandled and that you do not add too much water as this makes the pastry tough, and causes it to shrink a lot in cooking. When a recipe states 6 oz. ($1\frac{1}{2}$ cups) short crust pastry, it means pastry made with 6 oz. ($1\frac{1}{2}$ cups) flour.

Basic Cookery Terms

To bake blind: To bake a flan or pie without filling.

To baste: To spoon fat or liquid over food, usually meat or fish, during cooking to keep it moist.

To blend: To mix ingredients together, either solids or liquids.

To fold: To flick ingredients gently together in a figure of eight movement, so that no air is lost.

To marinate: To steep meat, fish or vegetables in a liquid containing acid, usually in the form of wine and lemon juice, which gives flavour and makes meat more tender.

Roux: The mixture of fat and flour used as the base for white sauce.

To rub in: To rub fat into flour with your fingertips until it looks like fine breadcrumbs.

To sauté: To cook in hot fat, tossing frequently.

To simmer: To cook below boiling point.

MEALS FOR ONE OR TWO

The recipes in this chapter are particularly designed for bedsitter cooks and for married couples who only want to cook for two people. Cooking in a bedsitter with only one, or maybe two, gas rings presents its own particular problems. Complete meals cooked in one pot, such as Pot-au-Feu (see page 42) and Vegetable Risotto (page 46) are the ideal solution when you have only one gas ring, and fresh French bread and tossed green salad are much more practical than traditional potatoes and a green vegetable. Green salads can become rather boring unless you vary them, so use different ingredients such as endive, Chinese cabbage, celery, chicory, green and red pepper, spring onions, mustard and cress, watercress and celery.

If you are preparing meat in a sauce, such as Devilled Kidneys (see page 38) and Barbecued Spare Ribs (page 46), when the meat is cooked it can be left in the saucepan and put on one side. Rice, noodles, small potatoes or a green vegetable can then be cooked, and whilst these are being drained, the meat can be put back on the gas ring for a couple of minutes to heat up again.

People often have difficulty in adapting recipes, generally intended for four, to serve just two. It is only too easy to halve the quantity of flour, for example, and forget to halve the quantity of liquid. It is much better to quickly write out beforehand the ingredients you will be using so that you do not go wrong.

Halving or reducing quantities in recipes is usually quite successful, but if you are making a stew or casserole, it is better to use just over half the quantity of liquid because of evaporation.

SOUSED HERRINGS (Birds Eye Foods Ltd.)

Soused Herrings

Soused herrings can provide a delicious, but inexpensive main course when served with salad, or they can be served as a starter. Mackerel can be treated in the same way as herrings.

4 herrings
salt and pepper
$\frac{1}{4}$ pint ($\frac{5}{8}$ cup) vinegar
$\frac{1}{4}$ pint ($\frac{5}{8}$ cup) water

1 tablespoon ($1\frac{1}{4}$T) mixed
pickling spice
3 bay leaves
1 onion, sliced

Cut off the heads of the fish with a sharp knife. Gently scrape the fish from the tail to the heat end to remove the scales. Slit the fish along the belly, slip out the roe and scrape the inside of the fish to remove the gut and blood vessels. Open the fish and place, skin uppermost, on a board. Firmly press all the way along the centre back of the fish. Turn the fish over and ease the backbone away from the flesh. Finally cut off the fins. Wash in salted water and dry. Season the fish lightly with salt and pepper and roll up from the head to the tail. Place in an ovenproof dish. Mix the vinegar with the water and pour over the fish. Sprinkle with the pickling spice, and add the bay leaves and sliced onion. Cover and bake in a slow oven, 300°F., Gas Mark 2 for about $1\frac{1}{2}$ hours. Remove from the oven and cool. Serve with brown bread and butter. Soured cream is excellent served with these herrings.
Serves 4 as a starter or 2 as a main course.

Hearty Vegetable Soup

This filling soup will make a meal in itself.

1 oz. (2T) butter or margarine
4 rashers (slices) bacon
1 onion, chopped
2 carrots, chopped
½ pint (1¼ cups) water
1 x 8 oz. can tomatoes

1 x 8 oz. can baked beans
pinch mixed dried herbs
salt and pepper
Garnish:
grated cheese

Heat the butter or margarine in a pan. Remove the rind from the bacon and chop. Fry in the hot fat with the onion and carrots for 5 minutes. Stir in the water, canned tomatoes with juice, baked beans, herbs and seasoning. Cover and simmer for 30 minutes. Sprinkle generously with cheese before serving and serve with crisp French bread.
Serves 2.

Mackerel Salad

few lettuce leaves
1 x 4½ oz. can mackerel fillets
3 tablespoons (3¾T)
   mayonnaise (see page 22)
1½ teaspoons horseradish
   sauce

few capers
2 gherkins, chopped
Garnish:
paprika
1 large, or 2 small tomatoes

Arrange the lettuce leaves on one or two plates. Drain the mackerel and place the fillets on the lettuce. Blend the mayonnaise with the horseradish sauce, capers and gherkins and spoon over the mackerel fillets. Sprinkle with paprika and garnish with quartered tomatoes.
Serves 2 as a starter or 1 as a main course.

Toasted Cheese with Bacon

This provides a quick and filling, but highly nutritious, snack. Toast a slice of bread lightly on both sides. Place a couple of rashers (slices) of bacon under the grill (broiler) with a halved tomato. Top the bread with two thick slices of good cooking cheese, such as Samsoe or Cheddar and cook until the cheese is brown and bubbling. As the cheese tends to run off the edge of the toast, it is quite a good idea to cover the grill (broiler) rack with a sheet of foil.

Serve the toasted cheese topped with the bacon and grilled (broiled) tomato and a few gherkins or dill pickles, if liked. **Serves 1.**

Avocado and Celery Starter

1 small avocado pear
2 teaspoons lemon juice
2 sticks celery, chopped
2 heaped tablespoons ($\frac{1}{2}$ cup) mayonnaise (see page 22)

few drops Tabasco sauce (optional)
salt and pepper
2 rashers (slices) streaky bacon

Cut the avocado pear in half and remove the stone, then peel. Cut the flesh into neat slices, then mix with the lemon juice in a basin. Add the celery, mayonnaise, Tabasco if using and season to taste. Turn into 2 small bowls. Remove the rind from the bacon and grill (broil) or fry until very crisp. When cool enough to handle, crumble roughly and sprinkle over the top of the avocado mixture. **Serves 2.**

TOASTED CHEESE WITH BACON (Photograph by Danish Agricultural Producers)

Cheese and Onion Potato Flan

1 x 2½ oz. packet instant
    mashed potato
2 tablespoons (2½T) flour
1½ oz. (3T) butter

1 large onion, chopped
¼ pint (⅝ cup) milk
2 oz. (½ cup) Cheddar cheese,
    grated
salt and pepper

Make up the instant potato following the instructions on the
packet. Add half the flour and ½ oz. (1T) butter. Form the potato
into a flan shape in an ovenproof dish or tin, building the sides up
well to hold the filling. Fry the onion in the remaining butter for
about 10 minutes. Add the last of the flour and cook, stirring, for
1 minute. Gradually stir in the milk and bring to the boil, stirring
all the time until thickened. Remove from the heat and add the
cheese. Season to taste and pour into the centre of the flan case.
Bake in a moderately hot oven, 400°F., Gas Mark 6 for 25 minutes
or until golden brown.
Serves 2.

Devilled Kidneys

2 large pig's kidneys or
    4 lambs' kidneys
1 tablespoon (1¼T) flour
salt and pepper
1 tablespoon (1¼T) butter or
    margarine
1 tablespoon (1¼T) oil

1 medium-sized onion,
    chopped
¼ pint (⅝ cup) water
½ beef stock cube
1 tablespoon (1¼T) mild
    French mustard
1 teaspoon Worcestershire
    sauce

Skin the kidneys. Cut the pig's kidneys into $\frac{1}{2}$-inch slices and discard the white cores, halve the lambs' kidneys and remove the cores. Season the flour with salt and pepper and toss the kidneys in this. Heat the butter or margarine and oil in a pan and fry the onion for 2 or 3 minutes. Add the kidneys to the pan, together with any excess flour and cook, stirring several times, for a further 10 minutes. Stir in the water and bring slowly to the boil. Crumble in the stock cube and add the mustard and Worcestershire sauce. Continue cooking for a further 10 minutes. Season to taste and serve with boiled rice or on hot buttered toast. **Serves 2.**

Fried Liver with Orange

1 tablespoon ($1\frac{1}{4}$T) flour
salt and pepper
grated rind of $\frac{1}{2}$ a small orange

4 oz. lambs' liver, sliced
1 oz. (2T) butter or margarine
juice of $\frac{1}{2}$ a small orange

Mix the flour with the salt, pepper and orange rind, then coat the sliced liver in this mixture. Heat the butter or margarine in a frying pan and fry the liver in the pan for about 5 minutes, turning once. Take great care not to over-cook the liver, as this spoils it. Pour the orange juice over the liver in the pan and mix well with the pan juices. Heat for 1–2 minutes, then serve. **Serves 1.**

Bedsitter cooks: If you wish to fry some vegetables to go with the liver, cook them first then push them to one side of the pan when frying the liver. Remove just before the orange juice is added.

Hamburgers

1 onion
8 oz. lean minced (ground) beef
1 egg yolk
seasoned salt and pepper*

or use ordinary salt and pepper

few drops Worcestershire
 sauce (optional)
fat for frying
1 tomato, sliced
2 soft baps (hamburger buns)

Slice the onion into rings, then finely chop two or three rings to give 1 tablespoon ($1\frac{1}{4}$T) chopped onion. Add to the beef with the egg yolk, seasoning and Worcestershire sauce, if using. Blend well then form into two flat cakes on a very lightly floured surface. Heat the fat in a fairly large frying pan and add the meat cakes to the pan with the onion rings. Fry the hamburgers for about 10 minutes, turning once. Turn the onions several times during cooking. Add the sliced tomatoes to the pan about 3 minutes before the hamburgers are cooked.

Split the baps (hamburger buns) and lightly toast, then place on one half a layer of onion rings, the hamburger, and the sliced tomato. Top with the other half of the bun. Serve with chips or potato crisps and salad.

Serves 2.

Note: It is not essential to add the egg yolk, but it helps to bind the meat together so that it does not break up during frying.

THE CLASSIC HAMBURGER (Photograph by Lawry's Foods Inc.)

Simple Pot-au-Feu

2 tablespoons (2½T) oil
1 onion, chopped
2 carrots, chopped
2 leeks, cleaned and chopped
2 sticks celery, chopped
8 oz. stewing beef
1 tablespoon (1¼T) flour

1 tablespoon (1¼T)
   concentrated tomato purée
½ pint (1¼ cups) water
1 beef stock cube
salt and pepper
1 lb. potatoes

Heat the oil in a pan and fry the onion, carrots, leeks and celery for about 5 minutes. Cut the beef into 1-inch cubes and fry with the vegetables for 5 minutes. Sprinkle over the flour and cook, stirring, for 2 minutes. Add the tomato purée, and gradually stir in the water. Bring to the boil, stirring all the time. Add the stock cube and seasoning. Cover and simmer for 2 hours. Peel the potatoes and cut into ½-inch slices. Add to the pan and cook for a further 30 minutes.

Serves 2.

To vary: Other vegetables such as turnips, peas and mushrooms could be used instead of those given here.
Use stewing lamb in place of beef.
Bedsitter cooks: These one-pot stews and casseroles are ideal if you have only one gas ring.

Cheese Soufflé

Contrary to popular opinion, soufflés are not difficult to make, and they can provide an inexpensive and delicious supper. For this quantity of mixture you need a 2-pint (5-cup) soufflé dish, but if you do not have a soufflé dish, any ovenproof dish of a similar capacity could be used, although if it is much shallower the baking time should be reduced.

4 oz. strong Cheddar cheese, grated
3 large eggs, separated
salt and pepper

$1\frac{1}{2}$ oz. (3T) butter
$1\frac{1}{2}$ oz. (3T) flour
$\frac{1}{2}$ pint ($1\frac{1}{4}$ cups) milk
$\frac{1}{2}$ teaspoon made mustard

Grease the soufflé dish well. Melt the butter in a saucepan, add the flour and cook, stirring, for 1 minute. Remove from the heat and gradually stir in the milk. Return to the heat and bring to the boil, stirring all the time until the sauce bubbles and thickens. Remove the pan from the heat and stir in the mustard and cheese. When the cheese has melted, beat in the egg yolks, one at a time. Season the sauce well with salt and pepper.

Whisk the egg whites stiffly until they form soft peaks, then, using a metal tablespoon, carefully fold the egg whites into the sauce mixture. This should be done in a figure of eight movement, so that as little air as possible is knocked out of the egg whites. Turn the mixture into the soufflé dish. Run the tip of a teaspoon round the outside of the mixture, scooping it up into the centre. Bake in a moderately hot oven, 375°F., Gas Mark 5 for about 30 minutes. Serve immediately.

Serves 2.

To vary : Add 4 oz. ($\frac{1}{2}$ cup) chopped ham in place of the cheese. Add the drained and flaked contents of a $7\frac{1}{2}$ oz. can of salmon, in place of the cheese.

Lemon and Ginger Chops

4 tablespoons (5T) oil
grated rind of 1 lemon
2 tablespoons (2½T) lemon
  juice
1 tablespoon (1¼T) brown
  sugar

1½ teaspoons ground ginger
salt and pepper
2 large or 4 smaller chump or
  loin chops

Mix the oil, lemon rind, lemon juice, brown sugar, ground ginger and seasoning together. Place the chops in a shallow dish and pour the marinade over them. Leave for 2–3 hours, or up to 36 hours, turning occasionally. Remove the chops and place under a hot grill (broiler). Cook for 15 minutes, turning the chops once and basting them with the marinade. Garnish with lemon and parsley if wished.
Serves 2.

LEMON AND GINGER CHOPS (Photograph by New Zealand Lamb Information Bureau)

Spare Ribs of Pork with Barbecue Sauce

1 tablespoon (1¼T) oil
2 spare rib pork chops
1 medium-sized onion, chopped
1 tablespoon (1¼T) concentrated tomato purée
2 tablespoons (2½T) water

1 tablespoon (1¼T) soft brown sugar
1 tablespoon (1¼T) vinegar
½ teaspoon Worcestershire sauce
1 teaspoon made mustard
pinch mixed dried herbs
salt and pepper

Heat the oil in a pan and quickly fry the meat on both sides until lightly browned. Remove from the pan and put on to a plate. Add the onion to the pan and fry gently for 5 minutes. Add the remaining ingredients, stir and bring to the boil. Replace the meat in the pan. Cover and simmer for 15 minutes.
Serves 2.

Vegetable Risotto

1 onion, finely chopped
½ small green pepper, chopped
2 oz. mushrooms, sliced
2 oz. (¼ cup) butter
4 tablespoons (5T) long grain rice

¼ pint (⅝ cup) water
½ chicken stock cube
salt and pepper
2 oz. cheese, grated

Fry the onion, pepper and mushrooms in the butter for 5 minutes. Stir in the rice and cook for 2 minutes, then add the water, stock cube and seasoning. Cover the pan and simmer gently for about 15 minutes or until the rice is tender and all the liquid is absorbed. Turn on to a serving dish and sprinkle with the grated cheese.
Serves 1.

To vary : Other vegetables e.g. carrots, peas, sweet corn, can be used in place of the pepper and mushrooms.
Cooked chicken, ham, chicken livers or shell fish could be used in place of, or as well as, the pepper and mushrooms.

Pipérade

2 red or green peppers
   (pimentoes)
8 oz. tomatoes
2 oz. ($\frac{1}{4}$ cup) butter
1 small onion, finely chopped

2 cloves of garlic, crushed
4 eggs
salt and pepper

Cut the peppers into $\frac{1}{2}$-inch pieces, discard the core and seeds. Peel the tomatoes. To do this either plunge the tomatoes into boiling water for a few seconds, then drain and peel, or hold each tomato over a gas flame for a minute or so until the skin "pops", then peel off. Cut the tomatoes into quarters and remove the seeds. Melt the butter in a pan and fry the onion, garlic and peppers gently for about 5 minutes. Add the tomatoes and continue cooking for a further 10 minutes.
Meanwhile beat the eggs in a basin and season with salt and pepper. Pour the egg mixture into the saucepan and cook gently over a low heat until the eggs are scrambled. Serve with hot toast.
Serves 2.

Veal Escalopes with Lemon

This is a good "special meal" for a Bedsitter Cook.
The veal only takes 15 minutes to cook, so any vegetables you may want to serve with the meat could be cooked before, kept hot in the saucepan in which they were cooked, then quickly tossed in butter and reheated at the last moment.

2 tablespoons ($2\frac{1}{2}$T) lemon
   juice
2 tablespoons ($2\frac{1}{2}$T) sherry
good pinch sugar
4 tablespoons (5T) single
   (light) or soured cream

1 oz. (2T) butter
1 tablespoon ($1\frac{1}{4}$T) oil
2 escalopes of veal
1 tablespoon ($1\frac{1}{4}$T) flour
salt and pepper

Heat the butter and oil in a frying pan. Lightly coat the veal with the flour seasoned with salt and pepper. Fry the veal for about 10 minutes, turning once. Remove from the pan and place on a serving dish. Add the lemon juice, sherry and sugar to the pan and heat for 2 minutes. Stir in the cream and heat *without allowing the sauce to boil.* Spoon over the veal and serve.

Serves 2.

To vary : Pork fillet (cook for about 15 minutes) or chicken breasts (cook for about 20 minutes) could be used in place of veal.

VEAL ESCALOPES WITH LEMON (Photograph by Jif Lemon Bureau)

Curried Chicken Vol-au-Vents

2 bought vol-au-vent cases
1 cooked chicken quarter
1 oz. (2T) butter
1 oz. (2T) flour
1 *level* tablespoon (1¼T) curry
   powder
½ pint (1¼ cups) water

1 chicken stock cube
1 tablespoon (1¼T) lemon juice
1 tablespoon (1¼T) red currant
   jelly
salt and pepper
3 tablespoons (3¾T) single
   (light) cream or top of the
   milk

Ready-made vol-au-vent cases can be bought from bakers and supermarkets. Put the cases into a moderate oven, 350°F., Gas Mark 4, for about 15 minutes or until heated through.
Cut the chicken into ½-inch pieces. Melt the butter in a saucepan, add the flour and curry powder and cook, stirring, for about 2 minutes. Add the water gradually and bring to the boil. Crumble in the stock cube, add the lemon juice, red currant jelly, seasoning and chicken pieces and heat gently for about 5 minutes until piping hot. Stir in the cream or top of the milk and season to taste. Spoon most of the mixture into the heated cases and the remainder round the bottom.
Serves 2.

Spaghetti Carbonara

2 oz. spaghetti
salt
$\frac{1}{2}$ oz. (1T) butter
2 rashers (slices) streaky
  bacon, de-rinded and
  chopped

1 tablespoon ($1\frac{1}{4}$T) chopped
  parsley
1 egg, beaten
pepper

Cook the spaghetti in boiling salted water for about 12 minutes or until *just* tender. Drain and rinse in cold water.
Melt the butter in the pan and fry the bacon for about 5 minutes. Add the cooked spaghetti to the pan with the parsley and a little pepper, then pour in the egg and mix well. Cook over a gentle heat, stirring well until the egg has scrambled. Turn on to a serving plate. Serve with a green salad.
Serves 1.

Apple Bake

1 oz. ($\frac{1}{3}$ cup) Cornflakes
1 tablespoon (1$\frac{1}{4}$T) desiccated
   coconut
grated rind of 1 lemon
$\frac{1}{2}$ oz. (1T) butter

1 lb. cooking apples
1 tablespoon (1$\frac{1}{4}$T) water
3 tablespoons (3$\frac{3}{4}$T) demerara
   sugar

Peel, core and slice the apples. Put into a saucepan with the water and 2 tablespoons (2$\frac{1}{2}$T) of the sugar. Cover and cook over a gentle heat until the apples are soft. Turn into two small ovenproof dishes. Mix together the cereal, coconut, remaining sugar and lemon rind. Sprinkle over the apples. Dot with butter. Bake in a moderately hot oven, 375°F., Gas Mark 5 for 20 minutes.
Serves 2.

Stuffed Peaches

1 x 14 oz. can peach halves
4 tablespoons (5$\frac{1}{4}$T) double
   (heavy) cream

2 tablespoons (2$\frac{1}{2}$T) chopped
   mixed candied peel
   (candied fruits)

Remove the peach halves from the syrup and put them into two individual dishes with the cut side uppermost. Lightly whip the cream until it just holds its shape, then carefully stir in the mixed peel (candied fruit). Put a tablespoonful of the cream mixture into the centre of each peach half. Finally pour over some, or all, of the peach syrup.
Serves 2.
Note: Fresh peaches can be used when in season. Halve, remove the stone and sprinkle with lemon juice to preserve the colour.

APPLE BAKE (Photograph by Kellog Co. of Great Britain Ltd.)

Pain Perdu

This is a rather simplified version of bread and butter pudding.

few drops vanilla essence
(optional)
about $\frac{1}{4}$ pint ($\frac{5}{8}$ cup) milk
2 slices stale bread, about
$\frac{1}{2}$-inch thick

oil for frying
1 egg, beaten
2 tablespoons ($2\frac{1}{2}$T) castor
(superfine) sugar
good pinch ground cinnamon

Add the vanilla essence to the milk and mix well. Soak the bread in the milk for about 5 minutes. Heat the oil in a frying pan. Quickly dip the bread in the beaten egg, using 2 spoons to turn it, then fry in the hot oil until the bread is crisp and golden brown. Turn once during cooking. Put the fried bread on two serving plates and sprinkle with the sugar mixed with the cinnamon.
Serves 2.

Banana Cream

$\frac{1}{4}$ pint ($\frac{5}{8}$ cup) natural yogurt
2 tablespoons ($2\frac{1}{2}$T) chopped
nuts (optional)

1 large banana
2 tablespoons ($2\frac{1}{2}$T) lemon
juice
2 tablespoons ($2\frac{1}{2}$T) honey

Mash the banana with a fork, then beat in the lemon juice and honey. Stir in the yogurt and most of the nuts and turn into 2 glasses. Sprinkle with the remaining nuts and serve.
Serves 2.

SUPPER DISHES

Finding a simple, not-too-expensive dish for supper, whether you are cooking for several people in a flat or having friends round for a casual meal, can be difficult. The recipes in this chapter are all inexpensive and filling, without being heavy. Savoury flans, such as the Dutch vegetable flan (see page 63) make very good economical main courses, and are an excellent way of using left-over pieces of chicken, ham, bacon and vegetables. Minced (ground) beef is usually a good buy and with additional ingredients a fairly small amount can feed a good number of people.

Kidney Kebabs with Barbecue Sauce

8 small onions
4 rashers (slices) streaky bacon
4 lambs' kidneys
4 skinless, or chipolata
   sausages
1 teaspoon concentrated
   tomato purée
1 teaspoon Worcestershire
   sauce
1 tablespoon ($1\frac{1}{4}$T) oil

For the Sauce:
$\frac{1}{2}$ oz. (1T) butter
1 onion, finely chopped
$\frac{1}{4}$ pint ($\frac{5}{8}$ cup) tomato ketchup
2 tablespoons ($2\frac{1}{2}$T) thin honey
2 tablespoons ($2\frac{1}{2}$T) lemon
   juice
salt and pepper

Cook the onions in boiling salted water for 4 minutes, drain. Cut off the rind from the bacon and stretch the rashers (slices) on a board, using the back of a knife. Cut each rasher (slice) in half and roll up. Remove the skins from the kidneys, halve and remove the white cores. Halve the sausages. Put the onions, bacon rolls, kidneys and sausages on 4 skewers. Mix the tomato purée with the Worcestershire sauce and oil. Brush this all over the kebabs. Put under a pre-heated grill and cook for 10 minutes, turning once and brushing with the Worcestershire sauce mixture during cooking.

Melt the butter for the sauce in a pan and fry the onion for 5 minutes. Add the remaining ingredients, bring to the boil and simmer for 5 minutes. Serve the kebabs with the sauce, boiled rice and courgettes and sweet corn, if wished.

Serves 4.

If preferred the kebabs can be served with hot garlic bread. Soften 2 oz. ($\frac{1}{4}$ cup) butter and beat in a crushed clove of garlic and some pepper. Take a French loaf and make cuts, about 2 inches apart, almost down to the bottom of the loaf. Gently pull the bread apart with your hands and spread the butter on to the bread between the cuts. Wrap the bread in foil and bake for about 10 minutes in a moderately hot oven, 400°F., Gas Mark 6.

Rice Cacciatori

For the Meat Sauce:
2 tablespoons ($2\frac{1}{2}$T) oil
2 rashers (slices) streaky
   bacon, de-rinded and
   chopped
2 large onions, chopped
2 cloves of garlic, crushed
1 lb. minced (ground) beef
1 x 14 oz. can tomatoes
1 tablespoon ($1\frac{1}{4}$T)
   concentrated tomato purée
$\frac{1}{2}$ teaspoon mixed dried herbs
salt and pepper

For the Rice:
2 tablespoons ($2\frac{1}{2}$T) oil
1 onion, chopped
1 green pepper, chopped
8 oz. (1 cup) long grain refined
   rice
scant $\frac{3}{4}$ pint ($1\frac{7}{8}$ cups) water
1 chicken stock cube
2 oz. salted peanuts
salt and pepper

For the meat sauce, heat the oil in a pan and fry the bacon, onions and garlic for about 5 minutes. Add the meat and cook for a further 5 minutes. Stir in the remaining ingredients, cover and simmer for about 1 hour. For the rice, heat the oil in a pan and fry the onion and pepper for about 10 minutes. Add the rice and stir over a gentle heat for a couple of minutes. Pour in the water and crumble in the stock cube. Stir, cover and cook over a gentle heat for about 15 minutes or until all the liquid is absorbed by the rice. Add the peanuts, mix well and season to taste. Put the rice on to a large serving plate and pour over the hot meat sauce. Serve at once.
Serves 4.

Store-Cupboard Casserole

½ packet spaghetti sauce mix*
1 x 14 oz. can tomatoes
1 x 1 lb. can cooked ham
1 x 11 oz. can sweet corn,
   drained

half green pepper, chopped
1 x 5 oz. packet instant
   mashed potato

If you do not have any spaghetti sauce mix, fry a chopped onion in 2 tablespoons (2¼ T) oil for 5 minutes, add the tomatoes and a good pinch of mixed herbs, then simmer for 15 minutes.

Make up the spaghetti sauce mix with the tomatoes, following the instructions on the packet. Fold the remaining half of the packet over carefully and store in a cool dry place to use again. Dice the ham and add to the sauce, together with some of the jelly from round the ham. Do not add too much jelly or the sauce will become too thin. Stir in the corn and the pepper, if using. Turn the mixture into an ovenproof dish or casserole. Make up the potato following the instructions on the packet, but make it a little softer by adding some milk, so that it spreads easily. Carefully spread over the tomato mixture. Bake in a moderately hot oven 400°F., Gas Mark 6 for 20 minutes.
Serves 4.

Normandy Chicken

1 small roasting chicken
1 oz. (2T) butter
1 tablespoon (1¼T) oil
1 onion, chopped
1 clove of garlic, crushed
3 rashers (slices) streaky bacon, de-rinded and chopped

1 oz. (2T) flour
¾ pint (1⅞ cups) dry cider
2 eating apples
¼ pint (⅝ cup) single (light) cream
1 tablespoon (1¼T) chopped parsley

Cut the chicken into 4 joints. Heat the butter and oil in a large saucepan and fry the chicken on both sides until golden brown. Remove from the pan and put on a plate. You will probably find it easiest to cook 2 joints only at a time. Add the onion, garlic and bacon to the fat in the pan and cook for about 5 minutes, or until the onion is golden. Stir in the flour and cook for 1 minute. Gradually stir in the cider and bring to the boil. Return the chicken to the pan, cover and simmer gently for 30 minutes. Core and dice the apples and stir into the chicken with the cream. Heat for 1–2 minutes without boiling, then turn into a heated serving dish and sprinkle with chopped parsley.
Serves 4.

NORMANDY CHICKEN (Photograph by Fruit Producers' Council)

Devilled Potato Salad with Frankfurters

1 lb. canned or cooked new
  potatoes
6 tablespoons (7½T) French
  dressing (see page 23)
1 small clove of garlic,
  crushed (optional)
2 teaspoons French mustard
dash Worcestershire sauce
pinch cayenne pepper

3 tomatoes
½ green pepper
6 spring onions (scallions),
  chopped
salt and pepper
paprika
8 frankfurters or other
  sausages

Scrub or scrape the potatoes and cook in boiling salted water until tender, or heat canned potatoes. While the potatoes are cooking mix the French dressing with garlic, if used, mustard, Worcestershire sauce and cayenne pepper. Drain the potatoes, cut into dice if large or leave whole if small and mix with French dressing while still warm. Allow to cool. Put the tomatoes and green pepper into a bowl, cover with boiling water, leave for 1 minute and drain. Peel the tomatoes and chop, removing the seeds. Remove core and seeds from pepper and chop. Add the spring onions (scallions), tomatoes and pepper to the potatoes. Adjust the seasoning, pile on to an oval plate and sprinkle with paprika. Split the frankfurters in half lengthways and arrange round the potato mixture.

Serves 4.

Dutch Leek and Mushroom Flan

6 oz. (1½ cups) short crust
pastry (see page 30)
2 medium-sized leeks
1 oz. (2T) butter
4 oz. mushrooms, sliced

salt and pepper
2 eggs
¼ pint (⅝ cup) milk
6 oz. (1½ cups) Gouda or Edam
   cheese, grated

Make up the pastry, roll out and use to line an 8-inch flan ring or tin. Bake blind (see page 28).

Trim off the top and root of the leeks. Slice the leeks into ½-inch rings and wash thoroughly. Heat the butter in a pan, add the leeks, cover and cook gently for 10 minutes. Add the mushrooms and seasoning and cook for a further 5 minutes. Remove the vegetables from the pan with a draining spoon or fish slice, so that any liquid is left in the pan, and place in the flan case. Beat the eggs with the milk and season well with salt and pepper. Add the cheese and spoon over the vegetables. Bake in a moderate oven, 350°F., Gas Mark 4 for about 30 minutes or until the top is golden brown.

Serves 4.

To vary : Omit the leeks and mushrooms and put 4 rashers (slices) of de-rinded and chopped bacon into the cooked flan case.

Omit the leeks and mushrooms and use 1 large onion instead.

Savoury Stuffed Pancakes

For the Batter:
4 oz. (1 cup) flour
salt
1 egg
$\frac{1}{2}$ pint (1$\frac{1}{4}$ cups) milk
fat for frying
For the Sauce:
1 x 7$\frac{1}{2}$ oz. can pink salmon
4 spring onions (scallions),
   chopped

2-inch piece cucumber,
   chopped
1 pint (2$\frac{1}{2}$ cups) white sauce
   (see page 23)
salt and pepper
4 oz. (1 cup) Cheddar cheese,
   grated

Sift the flour and salt into a large bowl. Add the egg and half the milk and mix to a smooth paste using a balloon whisk or a wooden spoon. Gradually beat in the remaining milk.

Lightly grease a frying pan with oil or cooking fat (shortening). Heat until the fat is very hot, then pour off any surplus fat. Pour 2–3 tablespoons (2$\frac{1}{2}$–3$\frac{3}{4}$T) of the batter into the pan and quickly tilt the pan in all directions, so the batter covers the entire base of the pan. Cook until the underside of the pancake is golden. Gently turn the pancake over using a fish slice or palette knife. Cook until this side is golden. Turn out of the pan. When each pancake is cooked, pile the pancakes on to a plate, separating them with a piece of foil or greaseproof (waxed) paper.

Add the salmon, together with any juice from the can, the spring onions (scallions) and cucumber to half the sauce. Season well. Divide this filling between the pancakes and roll them up. Place the stuffed pancakes in an ovenproof dish. Add the cheese to the remainder of the sauce and pour over the pancakes. Bake, uncovered, in a moderately hot oven, 400°F., Gas Mark 6 for about 30 minutes or until the pancakes and filling are heated through.

Serves 4.

To vary: Other fillings can be used; the meat sauce in the Rice Cacciatori on page 58 makes a very good stuffing.

Trawlers' Pie

1 oz. (2T) flour
1 teaspoon anchovy essence
   (paste), (optional)
2 hard-boiled eggs, quartered
salt
1 x 5 oz. packet instant
   mashed potato

1 lb. smoked haddock fillets
$\frac{3}{4}$ pint ($1\frac{7}{8}$ cups) milk
pepper
1 bay leaf
2 oz. ($\frac{1}{4}$ cup) butter or
   margarine

Put the haddock fillets into a pan with the milk, pepper and bay leaf. Cover and simmer gently for about 10–15 minutes or until the haddock is cooked. Remove from the heat, drain the milk and reserve it and flake the haddock.

Melt half the butter or margarine in a pan, add the flour and cook for a minute, stirring. Gradually stir in the drained milk and bring to the boil, stirring all the time. Remove from the heat and add the anchovy essence (paste), eggs and haddock. Taste and adjust seasoning. Turn into an ovenproof dish.

Make up the potato following the instructions on the packet. You may find it necessary to add a little extra milk so that it spreads easily. Spread the potato over the top of the fish and dot with the remaining butter or margarine. Put into a moderately hot oven, 375°F., Gas Mark 5 and bake for about 30 minutes or until the top of the potato is golden brown.

Serves 4.

Bangers Bolognese

1 lb. pork sausages
1 oz. (2T) butter
1 tablespoon (1¼T) oil
1 large onion, finely chopped
1 clove of garlic, crushed
1 x 6 oz. can condensed tomato
  soup

1 x 15 oz. can tomatoes
1 tablespoon (1¼T) chopped
  parsley
salt and pepper
8 oz. spaghetti
grated Parmesan cheese

Fry or grill the sausages until cooked. Remove from the pan and, when cool enough to handle, cut each sausage diagonally into 4. Heat half the butter and all the oil in a saucepan. Add the onion and garlic and cook gently for about 10 minutes until the onion is lightly browned. Stir in the tomato soup, canned tomatoes, parsley and seasoning. Bring to the boil and simmer in an open pan for about 10 minutes, then add the sausages.
While the sauce is cooking, cook the spaghetti in boiling salted water for about 12 minutes or until tender. Drain and toss in the remaining butter. Turn the spaghetti on to a serving plate, spoon over the sauce and sprinkle with Parmesan cheese.
Serves 4.

Moussaka

1 lb. aubergines (eggplants), thinly sliced
oil for frying
2 large onions, thinly sliced
1 clove of garlic, crushed
1 lb. minced (ground) lamb
1 x 14 oz. can tomatoes
2 tablespoons (2½T) concentrated tomato purée
dash Tabasco sauce
salt and pepper
2 eggs
¼ pint (⅝ cup) single (light) cream
2 oz. (½ cup) Cheddar cheese, grated
1 oz. (¼ cup) Parmesan cheese, grated

Fry one-third of the aubergines (eggplants) in oil for 3–4 minutes, turning once. Remove from the pan and drain well. Repeat this with the remaining aubergines (eggplants). Fry the onions and garlic in 1 tablespoon (1¼T) oil until pale golden brown. Add the lamb and cook for about 10 minutes, stirring occasionally. Add the tomatoes, tomato purée and Tabasco sauce and mix well. Bring to the boil and simmer in an open pan for 20–25 minutes. Season with salt and pepper. Arrange alternate layers of aubergines (eggplants) and the lamb mixture in an ovenproof dish. Beat the eggs and cream together and stir in the cheese. Pour on to the moussaka and bake in a moderate oven, 350°F., Gas Mark 4 for 35–40 minutes until the topping is firm, well risen and golden brown.
Serves 4.

Salad Niçoise

1 large lettuce
8 oz. cooked French (bobby)
   beans
8 oz. (1 cup) small cooked or
   canned new potatoes
2 oz. ($\frac{1}{4}$ cup) black olives
3 tomatoes, quartered
1 x 7$\frac{1}{2}$ oz. can tuna

2 hard-boiled eggs, shelled
   and quartered
4 tablespoons (5T) French
   dressing (see page 23)
1 clove garlic, crushed
salt and pepper
1 x 2$\frac{1}{4}$ oz. can anchovy fillets

Wash the lettuce, dry and use to line a large salad bowl. Put most of the beans, potatoes, olives and tomatoes into a bowl with the drained and flaked tuna, eggs, French dressing and garlic.
Season well with salt and pepper and spoon into the salad bowl. Garnish the top of the dish with the reserved beans, potatoes and olives and the drained anchovy fillets. Serve with crusty French bread.
Serves 4.

Meat Loaf

1 tablespoon ($1\frac{1}{4}$T) margarine
2 oz. (1 cup) dried
   breadcrumbs (raspings)
2 lb. lean minced (ground)
   beef, or use 1 lb. beef and
   1 lb. pork or beef sausage
   meat
1 medium-sized onion, finely
   chopped

1 teaspoon seasoned salt*
$\frac{1}{2}$ teaspoon seasoned pepper*
dash garlic salt
$\frac{1}{4}$ teaspoon mixed dried herbs
2 tablespoons ($2\frac{1}{2}$T)
   concentrated tomato purée
1 egg

If you do not have any seasoned salt and pepper, use ordinary salt and pepper and add $\frac{1}{2}$ stock cube dissolved in 1 tablespoon ($1\frac{1}{4}$T) boiling water to the beef.

Grease a 2-lb. loaf tin with the margarine, then coat with some of the breadcrumbs. Put the remaining ingredients into a mixing bowl and mix well, using first a large fork and then a spoon. Pack the mixture into the loaf tin. Bake in a moderately hot oven, 375°F., Gas Mark 5 for $1\frac{1}{4}$ hours. Serve either hot or cold. If serving hot, allow to stand for 10 minutes before slicing. **Serves 6–8.**

MEAT LOAF (Photograph by Lawry's Foods Inc.)

Baked Stuffed Potatoes with Cheese

4 large old potatoes
2 oz. ($\frac{1}{4}$ cup) butter
4 oz. (1 cup) Cheddar cheese, grated

4 oz. (1 cup) cooked ham or inexpensive salami, chopped
salt and pepper

Lightly prick the potatoes with a fork. Put them into a moderately hot oven, 400°F., Gas Mark 6 for about $1\frac{1}{4}$ hours or until they are soft. Remove the potatoes from the oven, cut them in half and carefully scoop out the soft insides, leaving the potato shells intact. Put the potato into a basin and mash with the butter. Add most of the cheese and all the ham or salami and season to taste with salt and pepper. Pile back into the potato shells and sprinkle with the remaining cheese.

Return them to the oven for 20 minutes or grill (broil) them under a medium grill (broiler) for 10 minutes or until golden brown. **Serves 4.**

Chilli Con Carne

2 tablespoons ($2\frac{1}{2}$T) oil
1 large onion, chopped
2 cloves garlic, crushed
4 oz. streaky bacon, de-rinded and chopped

1 lb. minced (ground) beef
1 x 14 oz. can tomatoes
1 x 14 oz. can red kidney beans
4 teaspoons chilli powder*
salt

Chilli powder can vary considerably in strength – some brands are quite mild, but others are very strong and $\frac{1}{2}$–1 teaspoon would be plenty.

Heat the oil in a saucepan and fry the onion, garlic and bacon for 5 minutes. Add the beef, stir well and fry for a further 5 minutes. Add the remaining ingredients and blend well. Cover and simmer gently for about 50 minutes, stirring from time to time, until thick. Serve with hot French bread.
Serves 4.

Bobotie

1 tablespoon $(1\frac{1}{4}T)$ oil
1 large onion, chopped or
    8 oz. small onions
1 lb. lean minced (ground) beef
1 tablespoon $(1\frac{1}{4}T)$ flour
scant $\frac{1}{4}$ pint $(\frac{1}{2}$ cup) water
1 beef stock cube
2 tablespoons $(2\frac{1}{2}T)$ soy sauce
1 teaspoon curry powder
$\frac{1}{2}$ teaspoon dried mixed herbs
salt and pepper

3–4 bay leaves
2 eggs
$\frac{1}{2}$ pint $(1\frac{1}{4}$ cups) milk
For the Rice:
12 oz. $(1\frac{1}{2}$ cups) long grain rice
$1\frac{1}{2}$ pints $(3\frac{3}{4}$ cups) water
$\frac{1}{2}$ teaspoon salt
pinch saffron powder
    (optional)
4 oz. $(\frac{4}{5}$ cup) seedless raisins

Heat the oil in a pan and fry the onion for about 5 minutes. Add the beef and fry for a further 5 minutes, stirring once or twice. Add the flour and cook for 2 minutes, then gradually stir in the water. Bring to the boil, stirring, then add the stock cube, soy sauce, curry powder, mixed herbs and seasoning. Cover and simmer for 20 minutes. Turn the mixture into a casserole and add the bay leaves. Beat the eggs with the milk and pour over the meat. Bake in a very moderate oven, 325°F., Gas Mark 3, for about 30 minutes or until the top is golden. Put the rice, water, salt and saffron, if using, into a saucepan. Bring to the boil and stir once. Lower the heat, cover and simmer for 15 minutes or until the rice is tender and the liquid absorbed. Stir in the raisins just before the rice is cooked. Serve with the Bobotie.
Serves 4.

BOBOTIE (Photograph by American Rice Council)

Steak and Kidney Pie

1 oz. (2T) lard or dripping
(shortening)
1 large onion, chopped
1½ lb. mixed steak and kidney
1 oz. (2T) flour

scant ½ pint (1¼ cups) water
salt and pepper
1 x 14 oz. packet frozen puff
pastry, thawed

Heat the lard or dripping (shortening) in a pan, add the onion and fry for 5 minutes. Add the steak and kidney and cook, stirring, for 5 minutes. Stir in the flour, lower the heat and cook, stirring two or three times, for a further 10 minutes. Gradually stir in the water and add seasoning. Cover the pan and simmer gently, stirring from time to time, for about 2 hours or until the meat is tender. Remove the pan from the heat and allow the meat to cool. When cold, turn the meat into a pie dish or other suitable container with a wide rim. Roll out the pastry to an oval, just a little bit bigger than the pie dish. Cut a strip of the pastry about ½ inch wide. Damp the rim of the pie dish and place this strip all the way round. Damp the pastry strip and carefully place the rolled out pastry over the top of the pie dish. Trim off the edges of the pastry with a sharp knife. Laying the index finger of your left hand carefully on the top of the pastry, about ½ inch from the edge, "knock up" the edges of the pastry using the back of the knife held in the right hand. To flute the edges, push the thumb of your left hand towards the edge of the pastry (so making a rounded shape) and make a cut into the pastry with the knife held in the right hand. Roll out the pastry trimmings and cut into strips about 1½ inches wide. Cut out diamond shapes for leaves, and mark on veins with the tip of the knife. Damp the leaves and arrange in the centre of the pie. If liked the pie can be brushed with a little egg or milk before baking to give it a good golden shine. Bake the pie in a very hot oven, 450°F., Gas Mark 8 for 5 minutes, then lower the heat to 425°F., Gas Mark 7 for a further 15–20 minutes.
Serves 4.

STEAK AND KIDNEY PIE (Photograph by Birds Eye Foods Ltd.)

Spaghetti Milanaise

10 oz. spaghetti
salt and pepper
1 oz. (2T) butter
4 oz. mushrooms, thinly sliced
4 oz. (1 cup) cooked ham,
  chopped
4 oz. (1 cup) cooked tongue,
  chopped

1 x $2\frac{1}{4}$ oz. can concentrated
  tomato purée
generous $\frac{1}{4}$ pint ($\frac{5}{8}$ cup) water
$\frac{1}{4}$ teaspoon mixed dried herbs
1 tablespoon ($1\frac{1}{4}$T) chopped
  parsley
grated Parmesan cheese

Cook the spaghetti in boiling salted water for about 12 minutes, or until just tender. Drain and rinse in cold water.

Meanwhile melt the butter in a large saucepan and fry the mushrooms for 5 minutes. Add all the remaining ingredients except the parsley and cheese and season to taste with salt and pepper. Cover and simmer gently for about 10 minutes. Add the spaghetti, mix well and heat for about 5 minutes. Turn into a serving dish. Sprinkle with parsley and serve with grated Parmesan cheese.

Serves 4.

Apple and Mincemeat Flan

12 oz. digestive biscuits
  (graham crackers)
3 oz. ($\frac{3}{8}$ cup) butter
2 tablespoons ($2\frac{1}{2}$T) golden
  syrup
1 pint ($2\frac{1}{2}$ cups) thick custard
  made up as instructions on
  the packet or can

2 eating apples
lemon juice
2 heaped tablespoons (5T)
  mincemeat
2 tablespoons ($2\frac{1}{2}$T) apricot
  jam (optional)

Crush the biscuits (graham crackers) finely with a rolling pin. The easiest and cleanest way to do this is to put the biscuits into a polythene bag and then crush them. Heat the butter and golden syrup in a pan and when the butter has melted, add the biscuits (graham crackers) and mix well. Press the biscuit mixture into an 8–9-inch flan ring or loose-bottomed sandwich tin. Put into a cool place to set. Make up the custard, cover with a circle of damp greaseproof (waxed) paper and allow to cool; the greaseproof (waxed) paper will prevent a skin from forming on the top of the custard.

Remove the biscuit crust from the flan ring or tin. Spoon the custard into the centre. Core and slice the apples and dip in lemon juice to preserve the colour, then arrange round the top of the flan as shown in the picture. Heat the mincemeat for a few minutes to melt the suet, cool and spoon into the centre of the flan. If liked the apples can be brushed with warmed apricot jam, as shown in the picture, but this is not essential.

Serves 4–6.

APPLE AND MINCEMEAT FLAN (Fruit Producers' Council)

Crème Caramel

1 tablespoon (1¼T) castor (superfine) sugar
few drops vanilla essence
1 pint (2½ cups) milk

4 oz. (½ cup) granulated sugar
4 tablespoons (5T) water
4 eggs

Put the granulated sugar and water into a saucepan, preferably a heavy one, and heat slowly until the sugar has dissolved. Raise the heat and boil the mixture rapidly, without stirring, until it turns pale golden. Pour into an ungreased ovenproof dish; tilt the dish so that the caramel runs all over the base.

Whisk the eggs with the castor (superfine) sugar and vanilla essence. Heat the milk so that it is just warm and pour over the eggs. Beat well. Strain the mixture on to the caramel. Place the dish in a roasting tin containing 2 inches of cold water. Bake in a very moderate oven, 300°F., Gas Mark 2 for 1½ hours or until set. Remove from the oven, cool and then chill. Loosen the edges of the custard with a knife and turn out of the dish before serving. **Serves 4.**

Baked Bananas

2 oz. (¼ cup) butter or margarine
2 tablespoons (2½T) brown sugar

grated rind and juice of 1 small orange
juice of ½ lemon
pinch ground mixed spice
4 large bananas

Melt the butter in a pan with the brown sugar, orange rind and juice, lemon juice and mixed spice. Peel the bananas, split in half lengthways and put into a baking dish. Pour over the butter mixture and bake in a moderate oven, 350°F., Gas Mark 4 for 30 minutes. Serve with cream.
Serves 4.

SLIMMING

There are a few people who can eat what they like and never seem to put on weight, but most of us find that at some stage we have to go on a diet. You can either choose one of the specific diets, which must be rigidly adhered to, or you can follow a low calorie diet which is rather more flexible. The calorie chart here should help you to choose the right foods and, together with the recipes, make sure you lose a few unwanted pounds.

Calorie Chart

The figures are for 1 oz. food unless stated otherwise.

Meat and Poultry

Bacon, lean 92
Bacon, fat 175
Beef, lean good quality 60–90
Canned corned beef 66
Canned luncheon meat 95
Ham, lean 65
Lamb, lean 60–90
Lambs' kidneys 29
Pork 119
Pork sausage 97

Fish

Canned salmon 30
Herrings 67
Lobster, prawns (shrimp),
shrimps 14–16
White fish, cod,
haddock, plaice 20

Vegetables

Beans, runner and French 4
Beetroot 7
Brussels sprouts 5
Cabbage 5
Carrots 7
Celery 3
Cucumber 2–3
Mushrooms 5
Onions 6
Spinach 5
Tomatoes 5

Fruit

Apples 11–15
Apricots fresh 11
Apricots canned 25
Banana 22
Currants 69
Grapes 15
Melon 7
Orange 10
Peaches 10
Pineapple, fresh 10
Pineapple,
canned 20
Raspberries 5
Strawberries 6

Dairy Products

Butter or margarine 220
Cheese, Camembert 90
Cheese, Cheddar 120
Cheese, cream 230
Cheese, cottage 50
1 egg, 80
Milk, 1 pint ($2\frac{1}{2}$ cups)
fresh whole 360
Milk, 1 pint ($2\frac{1}{2}$ cups)
dried skimmed 135
Single (light) cream,
$\frac{1}{4}$ pint ($\frac{5}{8}$ cup) 310
Yogurt, $\frac{1}{4}$ pint ($\frac{5}{8}$ cup) 100

Miscellaneous

Almonds 170
Bread 69
Chocolate biscuits 145
Desiccated coconut 180
Ice cream 60
Jam 74
Sugar 112
White sauce 41

Creamed Cauliflower Soup

1 small cauliflower
1 onion, chopped
1 pint (2½ cups) water

1 chicken stock cube
1 tablespoon (1¼T) dried
   skimmed milk powder
salt and pepper

Remove all the stalk from the cauliflower and break into flowerets. Put into a saucepan with the onion, ¾ pint (1⅞ cups) water and stock cube. Cover and simmer for about 1 hour. Remove the pan from the heat and whisk hard with an egg whisk or fork to break up the pieces of cauliflower. Mix the milk powder with the remaining water and stir into the soup. Season to taste with salt and pepper. Reheat gently and serve piping hot. **Serves 2.**

Baked Eggs and Ham with Mushroom

4 oz. sliced cooked lean ham
1 x 10 oz. can mushrooms,
   drained
black pepper

4 eggs
salt

Very lightly grease a baking dish or tin. Put the ham and mushrooms into the dish or tin. Season with pepper. Cover the dish with foil and bake in a moderately hot oven, 400°F., Gas Mark 6, for about 10 minutes.
Remove the dish from the oven and break the eggs over the ham. Season with salt and pepper. Return to the oven and bake for a further 10 minutes or until the whites of the eggs are set. **Serves 2.**

Braised Beef Neapolitan

12 oz. good quality, lean
   braising steak
salt and pepper
8 oz. tomatoes

1 small onion, chopped
1 clove of garlic, crushed
1 bay leaf
pinch mixed dried herbs

Divide the meat into 2 steaks and cut off any excess fat. Season well with salt and pepper. Put under a hot grill for about 5 minutes on each side, so it becomes lightly browned. Place in a casserole. Skin the tomatoes; either hold on a fork over a gas flame and remove and peel when the skin bursts, or put into a basin, cover with boiling water for 1 minute, drain and skin. Chop the tomatoes and put into a basin with the onion, garlic, herbs and seasoning. Mix lightly and spoon over the meat. Bake in a moderate oven, 350°F., Gas Mark 4 for 1–2 hours or until the meat is tender. This will depend on the thickness and quality of the meat. Serve with cooked spinach or a green salad.
Serves 2.

Veal Fricassée

1 onion, chopped
2 carrots, peeled and chopped
2 oz. button mushrooms
$\frac{1}{2}$ pint ($1\frac{1}{4}$ cups) water
1 tablespoon ($1\frac{1}{4}$T) lemon juice

$\frac{1}{2}$ chicken stock cube
8 oz. pie veal
1 egg yolk
2 tablespoons ($2\frac{1}{2}$T) skimmed
    milk
salt and pepper

Put the onion, carrots, mushrooms, water, lemon juice and stock cube into a saucepan and bring to the boil. Cut the veal into 1-inch pieces and add to the boiling mixture. Lower the heat, cover and simmer gently for about 45 minutes, or until the veal is tender. Blend the egg yolk with the milk in a basin. Add 3 tablespoons ($3\frac{3}{4}$T) of the hot veal stock, then add to the pan. Stir, without allowing the mixture to boil, until slightly thickened. Adjust seasoning and serve.
Serves 2.

Devilled Chicken

3 tablespoons ($3\frac{3}{4}$T) chutney
1 tablespoon ($1\frac{1}{4}$T)
   concentrated tomato purée
$\frac{1}{4}$ teaspoon Tabasco sauce

$\frac{1}{4}$ teaspoon made mustard
salt and pepper
4 small chicken joints

Put the chutney, tomato purée, Tabasco sauce, mustard and seasoning into a basin. Mix well together. Brush the mixture over the chicken joints, or make two or three deep slits in each chicken joint and fill with the devilled mixture. Place in a roasting tin and cover with foil. Bake in a moderately hot oven, 400°F., Gas Mark 6 for about 45 minutes. Uncover and continue cooking for a further 10–15 minutes or until the chicken is tender.
Serves 4.

Liver Ragoût

1 onion, sliced
2 carrots, sliced
1 small turnip, chopped
scant $\frac{1}{2}$ pint ($1\frac{1}{4}$ cups) water
1 beef stock cube
2 teaspoons Worcestershire
   sauce

salt
8 oz. lamb's liver, thinly sliced
about $\frac{1}{4}$ pint ($\frac{5}{8}$ cup) skimmed
   milk

Put the onion, carrots, turnip, water, stock cube, Worcestershire sauce and salt into a saucepan, cover, bring to the boil and simmer for 30 minutes. Meanwhile cut the liver into thin strips and soak in a little skimmed milk (this removes the slightly bitter flavour from the liver). Drain the liver and add to the vegetables in the pan. Simmer for about 10 minutes or until the liver is tender. Taste and adjust seasoning.
Serves 2.

DEVILLED CHICKEN (Photograph by Tabasco Pepper Sauce)

Watercress Egg Salad

4 hard-boiled eggs
2 teaspoons dried skimmed
  milk powder
2 tablespoons ($2\frac{1}{2}$T) water

4 tablespoons (5T) finely
  chopped watercress leaves
few chopped capers (optional)
salt and pepper

Shell the eggs, halve them lengthways and remove the yolks. Mix the milk powder with the water, add to the egg yolks and mash well. Stir in the watercress and capers, if using. Season to taste with salt and pepper. Pile the yolk mixture back into the white cases and serve on a bed of mixed salad. The salad can consist of lettuce, cucumber, tomatoes, green peppers, radishes or other low-calorie salad ingredients.
Serves 2.

Cottage Cheese Stuffed Tomatoes

4 large tomatoes
salt and pepper
8 oz. (1 cup) cottage cheese

4 spring onions (scallions),
  chopped
1 stick celery, finely chopped
$\frac{1}{2}$ teaspoon made English
  mustard

Slice the tops off the tomatoes and scoop out the centres. Lightly season the cases with salt and pepper. Mix the roughly chopped tomato centres with the cottage cheese, spring onions (scallions), celery, mustard and seasoning. Pile the cottage cheese mixture back into the tomato cases and top with the lids. Serve on a bed of lettuce.
Serves 2.

Stuffed Peppers

2 green peppers
8 oz. (1 cup) *lean* minced
   (ground) beef
1 clove of garlic, crushed
1 small onion, finely chopped

2 oz. mushrooms, finely
   chopped
good pinch mixed dried herbs
salt and pepper
$\frac{1}{2}$ pint ($1\frac{1}{4}$ cups) tomato juice

Slice the tops, i.e. the stalk end, off the peppers and discard the core and seeds. Mix together the minced (ground) beef, garlic, onion, mushrooms, herbs and seasoning and put into the pepper cases. Cover with the "lids" of the peppers. Put the peppers into a saucepan and pour over the tomato juice. Cover the pan, put over a low heat and simmer for 1 hour.
Serves 2.

Baked Fish with Apple

2 whole trout, sole or plaice
1 large eating apple

2 tablespoons ($2\frac{1}{2}$T) lemon
   juice
salt and pepper

Place the cleaned fish in a baking dish. Peel, core and slice the apple and arrange over the fish. Spoon over the lemon juice and season with salt and pepper. Cover with a lid or foil and bake in a moderate oven, 350°F., Gas Mark 4 for about 25 minutes.
Serves 2.

Cottage Cheese Salad Platter

Cottage cheese is very low in calories and consequently is one of the best protein foods to eat on a diet. The salad platter in the photograph on page 93 shows that, with a little imagination, it can be very attractively presented; this would be a particularly good dish to serve if you are on a diet and entertaining.

The cottage cheese can be flavoured with chopped spring onions (scallions), mustard, capers or horseradish. It can be served on its own or with lean cold meat or ham, as in the photograph, and plenty of low-calorie salad ingredients, such as tomatoes, celery, green peppers, radishes, cucumber and beetroot.

Yogurt and Chive Dressing

$\frac{1}{4}$ pint ($\frac{5}{8}$ cup) low fat natural yogurt
1 tablespoon ($1\frac{1}{4}$T) chopped chives

1 teaspoon French mustard
salt and pepper

Turn the yogurt into a basin, then blend in the remaining ingredients. Serve with green salad.
Serves 4.

Danish Blue Dressing

2 oz. Danish Blue cheese, crumbled
salt and pepper

$\frac{1}{4}$ pint ($\frac{5}{8}$ cup) low fat natural yogurt

Combine the yogurt with the cheese and season to taste. This dressing can be kept in the refrigerator for several days.
Serves 4.

FROM TOP, CLOCKWISE: SALMON MOUSSE; COTTAGE CHEESE SALAD PLATTER, YOGURT AND CHIVES, BUCKLING WITH HORSERADISH CREAM, DANISH BLUE DRESSING, CHICKEN AND ASPARAGUS FLAN (Photograph by Eden Vale Ltd.)

Slimmers' Apple Snow

12 oz. apples
peeled rind of $\frac{1}{2}$ a lemon
1–2 cloves
4 tablespoons (5T) water

artificial liquid sweetener
1 egg white
ground cinnamon

Peel, core and slice the apples. Put into a saucepan with the lemon rind, cloves and water and cook gently for about 15 minutes or until the apple slices are soft and pulpy. Remove the lemon rind and cloves and mash the apples with a fork. Sweeten to taste with artificial sweetener. Allow to cool. Whisk the egg white until it forms soft peaks, then fold into the apple. Turn into a serving dish and sprinkle with cinnamon.
Serves 2.

Orange Jelly

2 teaspoons powdered gelatine
   (gelatin)
$\frac{1}{2}$ pint (1$\frac{1}{4}$ cups) canned
   unsweetened orange juice

1 large orange

Soften the gelatine (gelatin) in 2 tablespoons (2$\frac{1}{2}$T) of the cold orange juice in a basin (see page 27). Stand the basin over a pan of gently simmering water and leave until the gelatine (gelatin) has dissolved. Add to the remainder of the orange juice and mix well. Cut off the peel from the orange, using a sharp knife, then cut into segments, discarding all the skin and pith. Put the orange segments into 2 small bowls. Pour over the orange juice and leave in a cool place until set.
Serves 2.

ENTERTAINING

Even those people who hate cooking usually confess to quite enjoying cooking for a party. So that you really can enjoy the cooking (and the eating), it is best to choose dishes which cook very quickly, or which can be completely prepared ahead and just reheated or cooked before serving. Unless you are serving soup, it is easiest to have a cold first course and pudding, so that these can then be made well in advance and forgotten about.

The recipes in this chapter are mostly suitable for both buffet and dinner parties. All the puddings and all the starters, with the exception of the buckling, are suitable for both. As far as main courses are concerned, the test of whether the recipe would be suitable for a buffet party is whether or not you can eat it easily with a fork. Casseroles such as the Beef in Red Wine (page 110) are very suitable for hot buffet dishes, and the Chicken and Asparagus Flan (page 110) would make a good cold main course. Many of the recipes in the Supper chapter would also be suitable for a casual buffet, particularly the Savoury Stuffed Pancakes (page 64) and Chilli con Carne (page 74).

Tea is far from being the elaborate meal it used to be, but if you should want to try some baking, the three recipes given are especially easy.

Mediterranean Stuffed Tomatoes

4 large or 6 medium-sized
   tomatoes
salt and pepper
2 oz. ($\frac{2}{3}$ cup) fresh white
   breadcrumbs
1 medium-sized onion, grated
1 clove garlic, crushed

2 oz. mushrooms, finely
   chopped
about 8 blanched almonds,
   finely chopped
1 tablespoon ($1\frac{1}{4}$T) chopped
   parsley
1 oz. (2T) butter
8–12 olives

Cut the tomatoes in half and scoop out the insides. Season the insides with salt and pepper and turn the tomatoes upside down on a board or plate to drain while preparing the stuffing. Chop the tomato pulp finely and blend with the breadcrumbs, onion, garlic, mushrooms, almonds, parsley and seasoning. Pile back into the tomato cases. Put a small knob of butter on top of each tomato and place in an ovenproof dish. Bake, uncovered, in a moderate oven, 350°F., Gas Mark 4 for 15–20 minutes or until golden brown. Garnish each tomato with an olive before serving. **Serves 4-6 as a starter.**

MEDITERRANEAN STUFFED TOMATOES (Photograph by Angel Studios)

Mushrooms à la Grecque

$\frac{1}{4}$ pint ($\frac{5}{8}$ cup) water
juice of $\frac{1}{2}$ lemon
2 tablespoons ($2\frac{1}{2}$T) olive oil
pinch dried thyme
1 bay leaf

1–2 cloves garlic, crushed
1 tablespoon ($1\frac{1}{4}$T)
   concentrated tomato purée
salt and pepper
12 oz. ($3\frac{3}{4}$ cups) mushrooms

Put the water, lemon juice, oil, thyme, bay leaf, garlic, tomato purée and seasoning into a saucepan and bring to the boil. Wash the mushrooms, but do not peel. Slice if large, leave whole if small. Add the mushrooms to the pan, cover and simmer gently for about 5 minutes. Remove from the heat and chill. Serve with warm bread and butter.
Serves 4.

Buckling and Horseradish Cream

Buckling are whole smoked herrings, which become cooked during smoking; they are similar in flavour to smoked trout which could be used instead.

4 buckling
few lettuce leaves
2 tomatoes, sliced
parsley sprigs
salt and pepper

For the Sauce:
$\frac{1}{4}$ pint ($\frac{5}{8}$ cup) double (heavy)
   cream
1 tablespoon ($1\frac{1}{4}$T) red currant
   jelly
2 teaspoons grated horseradish

Slit the skin of the buckling along the backbone and gently pull it away from the flesh on both sides. Place the lettuce leaves on a serving dish and arrange the buckling on top. Garnish with the tomato slices and parsley sprigs.
Lightly whip the double cream so that it just holds its shape. Melt the red currant jelly in a small saucepan over a low heat, then carefully fold into the cream with horseradish and seasoning. Serve the sauce separately.
Serves 4 as a starter.

Easy Liver Pâté

about 6 rashers (slices)
   streaky bacon
2 bay leaves
8 oz. lamb's or pig's liver
1 small onion
8 oz. pork sausage meat

1 tablespoon ($1\frac{1}{4}$T) chopped
   parsley
1 clove garlic, crushed
1 egg, beaten
salt and pepper
2 tablespoons ($2\frac{1}{2}$T) sherry
   (optional)

Cut off the rind from the bacon. Place the bacon rashers (slices) on a board and, using the back of a knife, in a stroking motion, stretch the bacon. Place the bay leaves in the bottom of a small ovenproof dish (preferably a deep one with straight sides) and line the bottom and sides with the bacon.

Mince the liver with the onion, or chop very finely. Put the liver into a basin and add the remaining ingredients. Mash with a fork and then beat with a wooden spoon until the mixture is well blended. Spoon into the bacon-lined dish and cover with foil or a lid. Place the dish in a baking or roasting tin containing 1 inch of cold water. Put into a very moderate oven, 325°F., Gas Mark 3 and bake for $1\frac{1}{2}$ hours. Remove from the oven and put some heavy weights on top to press down the pâté (full cans can be used for this). Leave until cold. Turn out of the dish, slice and serve with French bread or toast and butter.

Serves 6-8.

Salmon Mousse

1 x 7½ oz. can red salmon
4 heaped tablespoons (½ cup)
    thick mayonnaise
½ teaspoon anchovy essence
    (paste)
¼ pint (⅝ cup) double (heavy)
    cream
salt and freshly milled black
    pepper

2 teaspoons powdered gelatine
    (gelatin)
6 tablespoons (7½T) water
To garnish:
cucumber slices
parsley sprigs

Mash the salmon, together with any juice from the can, in a bowl, with the mayonnaise and anchovy essence (paste). Lightly whip the cream, fold into the mixture and season to taste. Sprinkle the gelatine (gelatin) over the water in a basin and leave for 5 minutes. Stand the basin over a pan of gently simmering water and leave until the gelatine has dissolved. Carefully fold into the mixture. Turn into 6 small moulds, or into 1 large dish and leave to set. Turn out of the moulds, by dipping them into very hot water for just a few seconds, then inverting them on to a plate. If you lightly damp the plate, the mousse can then be moved on the plate easily after it has been turned out. Garnish with slices of cucumber and parsley.
Serves 6 as a starter.

Ratatouille

2 medium-sized aubergines
    (eggplants)
salt
2 onions
4 tablespoons (5T) olive oil

2 red or green peppers (pimentoes)
4 large tomatoes
2 cloves garlic
freshly milled black pepper
To garnish:
chopped parsley

Chop the aubergines (eggplants) into $\frac{1}{2}$-inch dice, leaving the skin on. Put into a colander or sieve and sprinkle with salt (about 2 teaspoons). Leave to drain for about 20 minutes; this removes the slightly bitter taste of the aubergines (eggplants). Chop the onions finely and put into a pan with the oil. Cook gently for about 10 minutes or until soft. Chop the peppers, discarding the cores and seeds and add to the pan with the aubergines (egg-plants). Cover and simmer gently for about 30 minutes. Peel the tomatoes, either by holding over a gas flame until the skin bursts, or by plunging into boiling water for 1 minute, then draining. Chop roughly. Add the tomatoes, garlic and peppers to the pan and cook for a further 15 minutes. Taste and adjust seasoning. Chill. Sprinkle liberally with parsley before serving. Serve with warm French bread and butter.
Serves 6.

Artichoke Soup

2 lb. Jerusalem artichokes
2 oz. ($\frac{1}{4}$ cup) butter or
   margarine
1 large onion, chopped
2 sticks celery, chopped
2 rashers (slices) streaky
   bacon, chopped
1 pint ($2\frac{1}{2}$ cups) water
1 pint ($2\frac{1}{2}$ cups) milk

2 chicken stock cubes
salt and pepper
pinch mixed dried herbs
4 tablespoons (5T) single
   (light) cream or top of the
   milk (optional)
To garnish:
chopped parsley

Peel the artichokes under cold water to prevent discolouration and chop roughly. Heat the butter or margarine in a pan and fry the artichokes, onion, celery and bacon for 10 minutes, over a gentle heat. Add the water, milk, stock cubes, seasoning and herbs. Cover and simmer gently for about 30 minutes or until the artichokes are soft. Sieve the soup. Reheat, adjust seasoning and add the cream or top of the milk if wished. Garnish with parsley.
Serves 6.

Courgettes (Zucchini) and Prawns (Shrimp)

1 lb. medium-sized courgettes (zucchini)
1½ oz. (3T) butter
1½ oz. (3T) flour

¾ pint (1⅞ cups) milk
6 oz. (1½ cups) strong Cheddar cheese, grated
salt and pepper
4 oz. (1 cup) shelled prawns (shrimp)

Trim both ends of the courgettes (zucchini) but leave whole. Put into a pan of boiling salted water and cook for about 10 minutes. Drain and allow to cool then cut in half lengthways. Put half the courgettes (zucchini), rounded side downwards, into an ovenproof dish.

Melt the butter in a pan, add the flour and cook, stirring, for about 2 minutes. Gradually stir in the milk and bring to the boil, stirring all the time. Add the cheese and season to taste with salt and pepper. Stir in the prawns (shrimp). Pour just over half the sauce over the courgettes (zucchini) in the dish. Top with the remaining halved courgettes (zucchini), rounded side upwards, and pour over the remaining sauce. Put into a moderately hot oven, 400°F., Gas Mark 6 and cook for about 20 minutes.

Serves 4.

Shoulder of Lamb Chasseur

1 shoulder of lamb, about 3 lb.
2 oz. ($\frac{1}{4}$ cup) butter or
   margarine
1 small onion, very finely
   chopped
8 oz. pork sausage meat
4 oz. (1 cup) shelled walnuts,
   very finely chopped or
   minced (ground)

1 tablespoon ($1\frac{1}{4}$T) chopped
   parsley
pinch mixed dried herbs
grated rind of 1 orange
salt and pepper
1 egg, lightly beaten

Either ask the butcher to bone the lamb for you, or do this yourself. Make a cut, following the line of the bone, on the underneath of the joint. Using a small, sharp knife, cut round the bones until they are completely free from the meat, then remove. (See below).

Melt 1 oz. (2T) of the butter or margarine in a small pan and fry the onion for 2–3 minutes. Mix with the sausage meat, walnuts, parsley, mixed herbs, orange rind and seasoning. Bind the stuffing together with the beaten egg. Lay the meat with the cut side towards you and fill with the stuffing. Using coarse thread or fine string and a large needle, sew up the joint, then tie in two or three places with string. This holds the stuffing in position and helps to keep the joint a better shape during cooking.

Spread the joint with the remaining butter or margarine. Place in a meat tin and roast in a hot oven, 425°F., Gas Mark 7 for 20 minutes, then lower the heat to moderately hot, 375°F., Gas Mark 5 for a further 1 hour 10 minutes. Baste the meat two or three times during roasting.

Serves 6.

Dry Chicken Curry with Yellow Rice

1½ oz. (3T) butter
1 large onion, chopped
1 green pepper (pimento),
    sliced
1 clove garlic, crushed
about 1 tablespoon (1¼T)
    Madras curry powder
1 teaspoon chilli powder
salt
4 chicken joints
water (see method)
4 tomatoes
2 tablespoons (2½T) yogurt

For the Rice:
1 oz. (2T) butter
8 oz. (1⅓ cups) long grain
    refined rice
1 teaspoon turmeric
few cloves
1 teaspoon ground cumin
salt
1 pint (2½ cups) water

Heat the butter in a pan and fry the onion, pepper (pimento) and garlic for about 5 minutes. Add the curry powder, chilli powder and salt and mix well. Add the chicken joints to the pan and brown quickly over a high heat. Lower the heat, cover and simmer gently for 1 hour. If using frozen chicken joints, you will probably not need to add any water at all, but if using fresh joints, add 2–3 tablespoons (2½–3¾T) before lowering the heat. Add the tomatoes to the pan 5 minutes before the end of the cooking time. Stir in the yogurt just before serving.

Heat the butter for the rice in a pan, and toss the rice gently in this for 5 minutes. Add the spices and salt and mix well. Pour in the water. Cover and simmer gently for about 15 minutes or until the rice is tender and all the liquid absorbed. Before serving the rice can be garnished with a few pieces of sliced cucumber, as in the picture. Serve the curry with the rice, sliced onion, peanuts, chutney and poppadums if liked.

Serves 4.

DRY CHICKEN CURRY WITH YELLOW RICE (Photograph by American Rice Council)

Chicken Supreme

1 oz. (2T) butter
few finely chopped
   mushrooms or mushroom
   stalks
2 sprigs parsley
1 small onion, finely chopped
1 oz. (2T) flour
$\frac{1}{2}$ pint (1$\frac{1}{4}$ cups) chicken stock
   or water and 1 chicken stock
   cube
2 teaspoons lemon juice
12 oz. cooked chicken, sliced

1 egg yolk
4 tablespoons (5T) double
   (heavy) cream
salt and pepper
For the Rice:
8 oz. (1$\frac{1}{3}$ cups) long grain
   refined rice
1 pint (2$\frac{1}{2}$ cups) water
1 teaspoon salt
2 tablespoons (2$\frac{1}{2}$T) chopped
   parsley

Melt the butter in a saucepan. Add the mushrooms, parsley and onion and fry very gently for 5 minutes. Stir in the flour and cook for 1 minute. Gradually stir in the stock or water and stock cube and bring to the boil, stirring all the time. Reduce the heat, cover the pan and simmer very gently for 30 minutes. Strain the sauce and add the lemon juice and sliced chicken. Heat the chicken through for about 5 minutes. Mix the egg yolk with the cream, then stir in 3 tablespoons (3$\frac{3}{4}$T) of the hot chicken sauce. Pour the cream mixture into the pan and heat *without boiling*.

Put the rice, water, salt and parsley into a saucepan. Bring to the boil and stir once. Cover and simmer for 15 minutes or until the rice is tender and all the liquid is absorbed. Put the rice round the edge of the serving dish and spoon the chicken and sauce into the centre.

Serves 4.

Somerset Pork

1–1¼ lb. pork fillet
2 tablespoons (2½T) flour
2 oz. (¼ cup) butter
1 large onion, finely chopped
6 oz. mushrooms, sliced
½ pint (1¼ cups) dry cider

salt and pepper
4 tablespoons (5T) double
  (heavy) cream
To garnish:
chopped parsley

Cut the pork fillet into 8 pieces. Place each piece between 2 sheets of greaseproof (waxed) paper, and beat with a meat hammer or a wooden rolling pin until it is ¼ inch thick. Coat the pork lightly with the flour. Melt the butter and fry the pork slowly for about 4 minutes on each side. Remove from the pan, drain well and keep warm. Add the onions and mushrooms to the pan, and cook gently until tender, but not brown. Stir in the remaining flour, and cook for a minute. Remove from the heat and gradually stir in the cider. Return to the heat and bring to the boil, stirring. Add the pork and seasoning, then stir in the cream. Heat for a further 2–3 minutes *without boiling*. Serve garnished with chopped parsley.
Serves 4.

Beef in Red Wine

$2\frac{1}{2}$–3 lb. lean braising steak
2 oz. ($\frac{1}{4}$ cup) butter or
  margarine
2 tablespoons ($2\frac{1}{2}$T) oil
2 large onions, chopped
2 cloves of garlic, finely
  chopped
4 sticks celery, chopped

6 oz. streaky bacon, de-rinded
  and chopped
3 tablespoons ($3\frac{3}{4}$T) flour
$\frac{1}{2}$ pint ($1\frac{1}{4}$ cups) red wine
$\frac{3}{4}$ pint ($1\frac{7}{8}$ cups) water
1 tablespoon ($1\frac{1}{4}$T)
  concentrated tomato purée
1 bouquet garni
salt and pepper

Cut the steak into 1-inch cubes. Heat the butter and oil in a large pan and fry the onions, garlic, celery and bacon for about 10 minutes. Add the steak and cook for a further 10 minutes, stirring once or twice. Stir in the flour and cook for 2 minutes. Gradually stir in the wine and water and bring to the boil, stirring all the time. Add the tomato purée, bouquet garni and seasoning. Cover and simmer gently for about 2 hours or until the beef is tender. Serve with Scalloped Potatoes with Onions (see page 111) and a green vegetable.
Serves 8.

Chicken and Asparagus Flan

6 oz. ($1\frac{1}{2}$ cups) short crust
  pastry (see page 30)
1 small onion, grated
4 oz. ($\frac{1}{2}$ cup) roughly chopped,
  cooked chicken
1 tablespoon ($1\frac{1}{4}$T) chopped
  parsley

1 x $10\frac{1}{2}$ oz. can asparagus tips
2 eggs
$\frac{1}{4}$ pint ($\frac{5}{8}$ cup) single (light)
  cream
salt and pepper

SOMERSET PORK (Photograph by Taunton Cider)

Make up the pastry, roll out and use to line an 8-inch flan ring. Bake blind (see page 28). Put the onion, chicken and parsley into a bowl. Drain the asparagus and reserve 7 tips for garnish. Chop the remainder and add to the chicken. Beat the eggs and the cream, then add to the chicken. Season well with salt and pepper. Spoon into the flan case and bake in a moderate oven 350°F., Gas Mark 4 for 30–35 minutes until set. Allow to cool, then arrange the asparagus tips on the top.
Serves 4-6 for a main course or 6-8 as a starter.

Scalloped Potatoes with Onions

3 lb. potatoes
1 lb. onions
salt and pepper

$\frac{1}{2}$ pint ($1\frac{1}{4}$ cups) milk
1 oz. (2T) butter or
    margarine

Peel the potatoes and cut into $\frac{1}{4}$-inch slices. Cut the onions into thin rings. Put a layer of potatoes into a large, ovenproof dish, season with salt and pepper and cover with a layer of onions. Repeat these layers, ending with a layer of potatoes, and seasoning each layer with salt and pepper. Pour over the milk. Dot the top with butter or margarine and cover with a lid or foil. Bake in a moderately hot oven, 375°F., Gas Mark 5 for about $1\frac{1}{2}$ hours. Remove the lid for the last 20 minutes of cooking so that the potatoes can brown on the top.
Serves 8.

Elizabethan Flan

6 oz. (1½ cups) short crust
    pastry (see page 30)
2 large, thin skinned oranges
2 tablespoons (2½ T) thin honey

¼ pint (⅝ cup) water
¼ pint (⅝ cup) double (heavy)
    cream
2 oz. (¼ cup) sugar

Make up the pastry, roll out and use to line an 8-inch flan ring or tin. Bake blind (see page 28). Wash the oranges and cut into thin slices; keep the peel on. Mix the honey with the water, add the sliced oranges and leave to soak for about 8 hours, or overnight. Put the oranges, with the honey syrup, into a saucepan and simmer gently for 25–30 minutes. Drain, reserving the syrup, and cool the orange slices.

Lightly whip the cream and spread over the bottom of the flan case. Arrange the orange slices attractively on the top. Add the sugar to the reserved syrup and heat gently until the sugar has dissolved. Bring to the boil and cook until the mixture is syrupy; this will take 3–5 minutes. Spoon carefully over the orange slices to glaze.

Serves 6.

Ginger Cream Roll

¼ pint (⅝ cup) double (heavy)
    cream
¼ pint (⅝ cup) single (light)
    cream
12 oz. ginger nut biscuits

3 tablespoons (3¾ T) brandy or
    whisky
1 tablespoon (1¼ T) castor
    (superfine) sugar
To decorate:
sliced crystallized ginger

Lightly whip the cream together until it holds its shape, then beat in the brandy or whisky and sugar. Put about 1 heaped teaspoon of the cream mixture on each biscuit and sandwich the biscuits together to make 2 long rolls on a serving plate. Spread the remaining cream all over the biscuits. Put into a refrigerator or cool place and leave for at least 3 hours. Decorate with slices of crystallized ginger.

Serves 4-6.

Cheesecake

6 oz. digestive biscuits (graham crackers)

2 oz. ($\frac{1}{4}$ cup) butter or margarine

2 tablespoons ($2\frac{1}{2}$T) soft brown sugar

4 eggs

3 oz. ($\frac{3}{8}$ cup) castor (superfine) sugar

grated rind of 2 lemons

juice of 1 lemon

1 lb. curd, cottage or soft cream cheese

$\frac{1}{4}$ pint ($\frac{5}{8}$ cup) soured or single (light) cream

1 tablespoon ($1\frac{1}{4}$T) cornflour (cornstarch)

To decorate:
fresh fruit

Crush the biscuits (graham crackers) finely with a rolling pin. The easiest and cleanest way to do this is to put the biscuits into a polythene bag and then crush them. Melt the butter in a pan, add the brown sugar and biscuits (graham crackers) and mix until well blended. Press the mixture into the bottom of an 8-inch loose-bottomed cake tin.

Beat the eggs with the sugar, lemon rind and juice. Add the cheese, cream and cornflour (cornstarch) and beat well. Pour into the cake tin. Bake in a slow to very moderate oven, 300–325°F., Gas Mark 2–3 for 1 hour. Turn off the oven and allow the cheesecake to cool in the oven for 1 hour (this prevents the cake from sinking). Remove from the oven and chill. Decorate with fresh fruit before serving.

Serves 8.

Orange and Pear Caprice

3 oz. ($\frac{3}{8}$ cup) sugar
$\frac{1}{4}$ pint ($\frac{5}{8}$ cup) water
1 x 6 fl. oz. can concentrated
   frozen orange juice, thawed

1 egg white
2 oranges
1 pear
lemon juice

Put the sugar and water into a saucepan and heat slowly until the sugar has dissolved. Remove from the heat and allow to cool. Stir in the orange juice (do not dilute this) and mix well. Turn into a small container and freeze in the ice-making compartment of the refrigerator for about 2 hours, or until it is barely firm.

Remove from the refrigerator, turn into a bowl and mash with a fork so that no large lumps remain. Stiffly whisk the egg white in a separate bowl and fold into the orange mixture. Spoon back into the container and return to the refigerator. Freeze until firm; this will take about 6 hours.

Remove the peel from the oranges, using a sharp knife, and divide into segments, leaving the orange segments free from skin. Peel, core and slice the pear and sprinkle with lemon juice to preserve the colour.

Scoop the water ice into glasses and decorate with the orange and pear segments.

Serves 4.

Note: If you are in a hurry use commercially-made water ice— either orange or tangerine flavour.

ORANGE AND PEAR CAPRICE (Photograph by Fruit Producers' Council)

Mocha Cream

6 oz. (6 squares) plain
   chocolate
3 tablespoons ($3\frac{3}{4}$T) coffee
   essence

4 eggs, separated
$\frac{1}{4}$ pint ($\frac{5}{8}$ cup) double (heavy)
   cream

Break the chocolate up into small pieces and put into a basin with
the coffee essence. Stand the basin over a saucepan of hot, not
boiling water, stirring once or twice until the chocolate has
melted. Care must be taken when melting chocolate that it does
not become too hot or, instead of melting, it will become a hard,
granular mass. If you think the basin may be getting too hot,
remove it from the pan for a minute or two. When the chocolate
has melted, beat in the egg yolks one at a time. Lightly whip half
the cream and fold in. Whisk the egg whites stiffly then carefully
fold into the chocolate mixture. Turn into a serving dish and chill
if possible. Lightly whip the remaining cream and put
teaspoonfuls round the edge to decorate the top of the pudding.
Serves 6.

Quick Lemon Syllabub

grated rind and juice of 1 large
   lemon
castor (superfine) sugar to
   taste

$\frac{1}{4}$ pint ($\frac{5}{8}$ cup) double (heavy)
   cream
2 egg whites

Put the lemon rind and juice into a bowl with the sugar. The
amount of sugar needed will vary according to the tartness of the
lemons, but should be about 1 tablespoon ($1\frac{1}{4}$T). Add the cream
and whisk the mixture using a balloon whisk or rotary beater
until it just holds its shape. Whisk the egg whites stiffly and fold
into the cream. Spoon into glasses and chill for at least 1 hour
before serving.
Serves 4.

Countdown for Cooking a Dinner for 6

Menu
Egg Mousse
Lamb Cutlets in Pastry Case
Caramelled Potatoes
Green Beans
Fresh Fruit Meringue Cake

The Night Before
Make the egg mousse
Grill the cutlets
Cook the potatoes (if using fresh ones)
Make the meringue and leave to cook overnight

The Morning Before
Take the meringue out of the oven and leave to cool

The Evening
Dinner at 8 p.m.
6.30 p.m. Lay the table
6.45 p.m. Decorate the egg mousse
6.55 p.m. Complete the meringue cake
7.10–7.30 p.m. Make the mushroom stuffing for the lamb cutlets, cover the cutlets with the pastry and put on a tray or tin ready for baking
7.45 p.m. Put the beans on to cook and cook the caramelled potatoes
7.55 p.m. Put the cutlets into the oven. Put the bread into the oven
7.58 p.m. Turn the vegetables into heated serving dishes and keep warm
8.00 p.m. Serve the egg mousse

Egg Mousse

6 hard-boiled eggs
1 tablespoon (1¼T) very finely
   chopped onion
1 tablespoon (1¼T) chopped
   parsley
½ teaspoon anchovy essence
   (paste)
4 heaped tablespoons (½ cup)
   mayonnaise

¼ pint (⅝ cup) soured cream or
   yogurt
1 x 10 oz. can consommé soup
2 teaspoons powdered
   gelatine (gelatin)
2 tablespoons (2½T) cold water
salt and pepper

Shell the hard-boiled eggs and chop finely. Add the onion,
parsley, anchovy essence (paste), mayonnaise, soured cream or
yogurt and two-thirds of the can of soup. Soften the gelatine
(gelatin) in the cold water in a basin, then stand over a pan of
gently simmering water until the gelatine has dissolved.
Carefully stir into the egg mixture. Season to taste with salt and
pepper. Turn into a serving dish and chill. Chill the remaining
consommé. When the consommé is set like a jelly, chop and use
to decorate the mousse. Serve with warm bread and butter.
Serves 6-8.

Caramelled Potatoes

2 tablespoons (2½T) granulated
   sugar
2 oz. (¼ cup) butter

1½ lb. cooked new potatoes or
   1 x 1 lb. 12 oz. can new
   potatoes and 1 x 14 oz. can
   new potatoes, drained

Put the sugar into a frying pan and cook over a gentle heat until it
just melts. Add the butter and mix with the sugar. Toss the
cooked potatoes in the sugar and butter and heat gently until
they are golden brown.
Serves 6.

Lamb Cutlets in Pastry Case

6 large lamb cutlets
2 oz. ($\frac{1}{4}$ cup) butter
salt and pepper
2 tomatoes
6 oz. mushrooms, very finely chopped or minced (ground)

4 oz. cooked ham, very finely chopped or minced
1 tablespoon ($1\frac{1}{4}$T) chopped parsley
1 x 14 oz. packet frozen puff pastry, thawed
2 egg yolks
2 tablespoons ($2\frac{1}{2}$T) water

Dot the cutlets with 1 oz. (2T) of the butter, season with salt and pepper and grill on both sides until tender. Peel the tomatoes, either by holding on a fork over a gas flame until the skin bursts, or by plunging into boiling water for 1 minute, then draining. Cut the tomatoes into quarters, remove the seeds and discard. Chop the tomato flesh finely and put into a basin. Add the mushrooms, ham, parsley and seasoning. Melt the remaining butter, add to the mixture and blend well.

Roll out the pastry and cut out 6 rectangles, large enough to completely cover the cutlets. Put a spoonful of the ham mixture on each piece of pastry and place a cutlet on top. Top with another spoonful of ham mixture. Beat the egg yolks with the water and use to brush the edges of the pastry, Fold the pastry over so that each cutlet is completely enclosed. Place the cutlets, with the joins underneath, on a baking tray. Any trimmings left from the pastry can be rolled out and cut into diamond-shaped leaves for decoration. Brush all over the pastry with beaten egg and bake in a hot oven, 425°F., Gas Mark 7 for about 20 minutes or until golden brown. Serve with French beans and Caramelled Potatoes (see page 118).
Serves 6.

Fresh Fruit Meringue Cake

4 egg whites

8 oz. (1 cup) castor (superfine) or icing (confectioners') sugar

$\frac{1}{2}$ pint (1$\frac{1}{4}$ cups) double (heavy) cream

about 1 lb. fresh fruit e.g. raspberries, strawberries, cherries or mixed fruit or 1 lb. 12 oz. can fruit, drained

extra sugar

Draw an 8-inch circle on a sheet of oiled greaseproof (waxed) paper. Whisk the egg whites until they are very stiff and you can turn turn the bowl upside down. Gradually beat in half the sugar, a teaspoon at a time, then fold in the remainder. Spread half the meringue over the circle, taking it right to the edges. Using a dessertspoon, pile spoonfuls of meringue all round the edge to make a case. Bake in a very cool oven, 200°F., Gas Mark $\frac{1}{4}$ for about 6 hours or until the meringue has completely dried out and the paper can be easily removed. The meringue case can be left in the oven to dry out overnight; turn the oven down as low as possible and cook for about 10 hours.

Whip the cream lightly until it just holds its shape. Spread over the base of the meringue case. Top with the fruit; fresh fruit will probably need to be sprinkled with a little sugar before serving. If using fruits which discolour, such as apples, pears and peaches, they should first be dipped in a little lemon juice to preserve the colour.

Serves 6.

Scones

8 oz. (2 cups) plain flour
½ teaspoon salt
1 teaspoon bicarbonate of soda
   (baking soda)

2 teaspoons cream of tartar
1½ oz. (3T) butter or
   margarine
about ¼ pint (⅝ cup) milk

Sift the flour, salt, bicarbonate of soda and cream of tartar into a bowl. Cut the butter or margarine into small pieces and rub these into the flour with the tips of your fingers. Bind the mixture with the milk to give a soft, but not wet, consistency, using a round bladed knife. Lightly flour a working surface and pat or roll out the dough until it is ½-inch thick. Either cut into squares or cut into 2-inch rounds, using a pastry cutter or top of a small glass. Place the scones on a baking tray and bake in a hot oven, 425°F., Gas Mark 7 for 10 minutes or until risen and golden brown. Serve warm with butter and jam.

Makes about 12.

Simple Fruit Cake

8 oz. (2 cups) self-raising (all-purpose) flour or plain flour and 2 teaspoons baking powder

pinch salt

$\frac{1}{2}$ teaspoon ground mixed spice

3 oz. ($\frac{3}{8}$ cup) butter or margarine

4 oz. ($\frac{1}{2}$ cup) castor (superfine) sugar

4 oz. ($\frac{1}{2}$ cup) raisins

4 oz. ($\frac{1}{2}$ cup) sultanas

2 oz. ($\frac{1}{4}$ cup) candied peel

1 egg, lightly beaten

about $\frac{1}{4}$ pint ($\frac{5}{8}$ cup) milk

Well grease a 7-inch round cake tin. Cut out a circle of greaseproof (waxed) paper the size of the base and place this in position. Grease well. Sieve together the flour, baking powder, if using, salt and spice. Cut the fat into about 8 pieces and using the tips of your fingers, rub this into the flour until the mixture resembles fine breadcrumbs. Add the sugar, raisins, sultanas and peel and mix well. Add the egg and sufficient milk so that the mixture will drop from a spoon when shaken. Spoon into the cake tin. Bake in a moderately hot oven, 375°F., Gas Mark 5 for about 1 hour or until the cake is golden brown and a skewer put into the centre comes out clean. Turn out and cool on a wire rack.

Quick Mix Chocolate Cake

2 heaped tablespoons (4T)
  cocoa
2 tablespoons (2½T) hot water
6 oz. (1½ cups) self-raising
  (all-purpose) flour
1½ teaspoons baking powder
6 oz. (¾ cup) soft margarine
6 oz. (¾ cup) castor (superfine)
  sugar
2 large eggs

For the Filling:
1 tablespoon (1¼T) cocoa
1 tablespoon (1¼T) hot water
2 oz. (¼ cup) butter or
  margarine
4 oz. (½ cup) sifted icing
  (confectioners') sugar

Grease two 7-inch sandwich tins with margarine. Cut out two circles of greaseproof paper the size of the bottom of the tins and place in position. Grease these with margarine.

Blend the cocoa with the hot water, put into a mixing bowl and allow to cool. Sift the flour with the baking powder into a bowl and add the remaining ingredients. Beat well with a wooden spoon for 2–3 minutes until the mixture is well blended. Turn into the prepared cake tins and bake in a very moderate oven, 325°F., Gas Mark 3 for 25–35 minutes or until the cakes spring back when lightly touched. Turn out and cool on a wire rack. Blend the cocoa for the icing with the hot water and allow to cool. Beat the butter or margarine and gradually beat in half the icing (confectioners') sugar. Add the chocolate mixture and beat in the remaining icing (confectioners') sugar. When the cakes are cold spread the filling over the top of one of the cakes and place the second cake on top.

INDEX